USA TODAY'S DEBATE: VOICES AND PERSPECTIVES

GENETIC ENGINEERING

Modern Progress or Future Peril?

Linda Tagliaferro

Twenty-First Century Books · Minneapolis

Twenty-First Century Books
A division of Lerner Publishing Group, Inc.
241 First Avenue North
Minneapolis, MN 55401 U.S.A.

Website address: www.lernerbooks.com

The publisher wishes to thank Ben Nussbaum and Phil Pruitt of USA TODAY for their help in
preparing this book.

Library of Congress Cataloging-in-Publication Data

Tagliaferro, Linda.
    Genetic engineering : modern progress or future peril? / by Linda Tagliaferro.
      p. cm. — (USA today's debate: voices and perspectives)
    Includes bibliographical references and index.
    ISBN 978–0–7613–4081–2 (lib. bdg. : alk. paper)
    1. Genetic engineering. 2. Genetic engineering—Moral and ethical aspects. I. Title.
QH442.T3258 2010
174'.957—dc22   2009004271

Manufactured in the United States of America
1 2 3 4 5 6 – DP – 15 14 13 12 11 10

CONTENTS

Introduction

Imagine a world where there is no hunger—a world where cancer, AIDS (acquired immunodeficiency syndrome), and other dreaded diseases no longer impair human lives. Imagine a world where people can choose exactly what their children will look like and how intelligent they will be. This may sound like science fiction. But recent advances in a technology called genetic engineering have led some people to predict that these changes and others like them may come about in the not-so-distant future.

Genetic engineering—also called gene-splicing, or gene cloning—has made it possible for scientists to manipulate genes, the basic units of heredity. The cells of all living organisms contain genes. Genes carry chemical information that helps determine many of an organism's characteristics. By changing the genes of an organism, scientists can give the organism different traits. Many scientists think they can alter human evolution as well as that of plants and animals. Cloning, another genetic technology, seeks to make an exact copy of all the genes in a plant, animal, or human.

Left: A biologist at the U.S. Centers for Disease Control and Prevention prepares for an experiment that uses genetic material. Manipulating genes is a reality of the twenty-first century.

Stem cell therapy, a technology that relies on the properties of special cells to potentially grow into any type of cell, may cure diseases such as cancer and Alzheimer's disease in the future. Perhaps stem cell therapy will repair failing organs such as hearts and livers.

Supporters of these genetic technologies point out the many potential advantages. Increased food production, revolutionary new medicines, and even enhanced human intelligence, physical beauty, and strength are just some potential advantages.

Opponents, however, argue that the dangers outweigh the benefits. They caution that we know too little about these technologies and their long-term effects. Will the future bring a race of made-to-order humans who have lost forever the great gift of genetic diversity? Is it ethical to create new animals to use as medicine factories or organ donors for humans? Is it right for corporations to own human genes? Is it ethical to

Above: Some opponents of genetic technologies take to the streets of Washington, D.C., to make their opinion known in 2007. These costumed protesters are speaking out against cloned animals as a source of food for humans.

grow human embryos for stem cells that might one day cure human diseases when doing so involves the destruction of those embryos? Will genetic engineering be misused in the hands of the economically or politically powerful? Once genetic engineering and other genetic technologies become widespread, opponents warn, there will be no turning back. They compare it to other technologies, such as chemical pesticides and nuclear energy, which were welcomed in their early stages. But many of these technologies were later revealed to have dangerous side effects that still threaten us.

OPPOSING VIEW

On the other hand, this advanced technology does exist. Is it right to halt research that has the potential to save lives and improve the environment? Should experiments in human gene therapy be stopped when they might bring about cures for devastating diseases that continue to plague humankind? Should the manufacture of genetically engineered hormones be discontinued—even if it means depriving those who desperately need them? Will the opportunity to develop vaccines that could conquer AIDS and other disorders be lost? Should human cloning be banned when it might be the only way for some childless couples to have children?

For better or worse, genetic engineering and other genetic technologies will affect the environment and food supply. These technologies will ultimately change the way we think about medicine. As the "age of genetics" unfolds, keep in mind the words of the late senator J. William Fulbright of Arkansas. He cautioned years ago that "science has radically changed the conditions of human life on Earth. It has expanded our knowledge and our power, but not our capacity to use them with wisdom." The "genetic revolution" is already changing our lives. A thorough examination of these issues will help explain how this powerful scientific technology can be developed responsibly and show us what we need to do to voice our concerns.

CHAPTER ONE

What Is Genetic Engineering?

All living things—flowers, trees, animals, and people—are made of cells, the basic units of life. Some organisms have only one cell. The human body, however, has trillions of cells. Cells are so small that they can be seen only under a microscope. In plants and animals, cells have specific jobs to do. For example, nerve cells in your eyes are carrying messages to your brain as you read this book. Muscle cells move your eyes across the page. Specialized cells group together to form tissues. Different kinds of tissues form organs, such as the eyes, the heart, and the lungs.

Although cells do different jobs, all cells have some things in common. All cells are alive. They reproduce (create their own kind), and they die. A thin cover, called the cell wall, encloses each cell. Inside the cover is a jellylike fluid called cytoplasm. The fluid contains many tiny structures. One of these structures is the nucleus. It is the cell's control center. The nucleus contains the cell's genetic program. The program is a master plan that controls almost everything the cell does. The nucleus contains two kinds of structures—chromosomes and nucleoli. Chromosomes are threadlike structures. They consist of a chemical substance

Left: This young man, tree, dog, and all other living things are made of cells. Genetic engineers modify the control center of cells to force changes.

called DNA (deoxyribonucleic acid) and certain proteins. Nucleoli are round bodies that form in certain regions of specific chromosomes.

Every new cell is produced from an existing cell. Cells reproduce by dividing. When a cell divides, each of the two new cells gets a copy of the genetic program. The genetic program carried in DNA makes each living thing different from every other living thing. That's why DNA is sometimes called the code of life. DNA tells cells how to produce exact copies of themselves. Those new cells, in turn, follow the DNA's instructions to duplicate themselves.

DNA molecules are tightly coiled in the chromosomes of cells. The molecules look like twisted rope ladders. All DNA molecules are shaped this way, whether they come from a flower, a dog, or a human being. Long threads make up the sides of the ladder, and the rungs are made up of pairs of four compounds called bases. The bases are adenine, cytosine, guanine, and thymine (abbreviated A,

C, G, and T). Because of their unique compositions, A can only pair with T and C with G. When these chemicals bond, they are called base pairs. Each rung of the ladder consists of a base pair. The loosely formed base pair bonds can split apart like a molecular zipper and then pair up with more bases to reproduce exact copies of themselves.

A pattern of bases, such as ATCGAT, forms along each rung of the ladder. Hundreds, thousands, or even millions of these bases form sections of DNA called genes. Genes determine characteristics that living things have. Human cells contain about twenty to twenty-five thousand genes. They are made up of more than three billion base pairs—pairs of As, Cs, Ts, and Gs—all in a specific order. When cells reproduce, occasionally an error occurs in the reproduction of their DNA. An A, for example, is copied instead of a C or a G instead of a T. These errors are mutations—permanent changes in the DNA. A mutation causes the production of a protein that is different from the original one. If the mutated genes are present in the organism's sex cells, they will be transmitted to the offspring. Some mutations can be fatal. But others produce a newer, stronger, better-equipped organism than the original "correct" one. In the process of genetic engineering, scientists add or delete whole sections of DNA in cells to produce specific, intended changes in living organisms.

A BRIEF HISTORY OF GENETICS

Scientists made several landmark discoveries about genetics during the nineteenth and twentieth centuries. The study of heredity—the way in which traits are passed from one generation to the next—began with an Austrian monk named Gregor Mendel (1822–1884). Mendel was an amateur gardener. Working in a monastery in Brünn (modern-day Brno in the Czech Republic), he noticed that some pea plants produced offspring that had smooth, round peas. Other peas were rough and wrinkled. There were short plants as well as tall varieties, yellow peas as well as green ones.

Mendel spent seven years carefully observing how characteristics were transferred from one generation to the

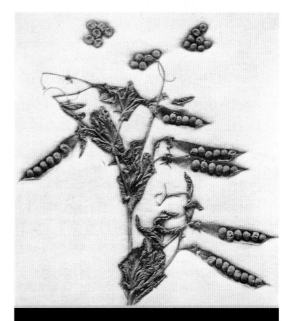

This illustration shows the results that Gregor Mendel observed from crossing yellow wrinkled peas *(top left)* and green round peas *(top right)*. The first generation resulted in yellow wrinkled peas *(top center)*. The second generation had a mix of pea characteristics *(peas in pods)*.

www.usatoday.com

USA TODAY

Life

SECTION D

February 24, 2003

Life-changing science began with humble pea

From the Pages of
USA TODAY

Major advances rarely come out of the blue; they build on discoveries that preceded them. The story of how scientists unraveled the structure of DNA was built on work that started more than 100 years earlier.

It wasn't until the 1850s that Austrian monk Gregor Mendel worked out the basics of heredity during an eight-year, meticulously recorded experiment involving the hybridization of more than 30,000 sweet peas.

Scientists had seen chromosomes in cells since the 1840s, but no one understood what they were. Deoxyribonucleic acid, or DNA, was itself isolated in 1869, but again, no one knew what it did. . . .

At the beginning of the twentieth century, Mendel's work was rediscovered, and in 1909 those hereditary units were called "genes."

—Elizabeth Weise

next. He concluded that certain principles or "factors" determine whether a plant's offspring will be tall or short, wrinkled or smooth. He also discovered that the offspring receives two copies of each factor, one from each parent. He noted that some factors were dominant over others. Rather than the stronger and weaker traits blending, the dominant factor showed up in the offspring. We call Mendel's "factors" genes. In 1865 Mendel presented his theories to the local science society in Brünn. But his ideas were not accepted as the brilliant discoveries that they were. When Mendel died in 1884, little of his work was remembered. In 1900, however, three scientists, working independently in three different countries, came to the same conclusions about heredity that Mendel had. These men were Hugo de Vries in the Netherlands, Karl Correns in Germany, and Erich von Tschermak in Austria. Eventually, each scientist credited Mendel as the true discoverer of the principles of heredity.

UNRAVELING THE MYSTERIES OF THE DOUBLE HELIX

In the twentieth century, scientists discovered more about heredity, especially about DNA. In the 1920s, Fred Griffith, a British microbiologist (someone who studies microscopic forms of life), studied two strains, or types, of *pneumococcus*. That is the bacteria that can cause pneumonia. One strain has a smooth outer coating on its cells. The other has a rough outer coating. When Griffith injected the smooth strain into laboratory mice, they developed pneumonia and died. An injection of the strain with the rough outer coating, however, did not harm the mice. Griffith then killed some of the smooth strain bacteria and injected them into mice. The animals lived, and the scientist concluded that killing the bacteria rendered them harmless. An unexpected development took place, however. When Griffith took the dead, smooth strain of bacteria and injected it into mice along with the harmless, live, rough strain of bacteria, the animals died. In 1928 Griffith concluded that something in the dead, harmful strain had changed the harmless strain into a deadly one. In the 1940s, Oswald T. Avery and a team of researchers at Rockefeller University in New York City tried to determine just what had caused that change. In 1944, after years of experiments based on Griffith's findings, Avery and his team announced that the changing, or transforming, substance was DNA.

Spurred on by these developments, other scientists began to study DNA. Scientists already understood many facts about its composition. But no one knew the molecule's exact structure. DNA was too small to be photographed by normal means. It could not even be viewed through a microscope. In the early 1950s, however, Maurice Wilkins and Rosalind Franklin, working at King's College in

Cambridge, England, used X-ray diffraction photography to study DNA. This type of photography does not produce the kind of picture that comes from a regular camera. Instead, it makes an outline of the objects by passing X-rays through them.

Using all these intriguing yet incomplete clues, James Watson, an American, and Francis Crick, an Englishman, built three-dimensional models of possible structures for this molecule. Their model was based on the X-ray diffraction photographs of Wilkins and Franklin. Working at Cambridge University in Britain, the team came up with the concept of a double helix. This shape looks like two spiral staircases wound around each other,

or like a twisted ladder. The ladder's "rungs" were made up of the nucleotide bases—adenine, thymine, cytosine, and guanine. On April 25, 1953, Watson and Crick announced their findings in *Nature*, a respected British journal. In 1962 Watson, Crick, and Wilkins won the Nobel Prize in Physiology or Medicine. (Rosalind Franklin, who had contributed so much to this discovery, died before she could be awarded this honor. The prize is awarded only to living people.)

In 1970 Hamilton Smith and Daniel Nathans discovered in bacteria a class of naturally occurring enzymes. Enzymes are proteins whose function is to destroy foreign DNA such as that from invading viruses. These are

❝Although a [scientific] paper by Oswald Avery in 1944 suggested that genes were in fact made of DNA, it wasn't until 1952 that biologists proved it.❞

—ELIZABETH WEISE,
USA TODAY FEBRUARY 24, 2003

> ❝ **An unlikely pair of researchers, geneticist James Watson and biologist Francis Crick, teamed up at a laboratory in Cambridge, England. Watson was brilliant, scraggly, shrewd, and very American. Crick was well dressed, very British, and equally brilliant.** ❞

—ELIZABETH WEISE,
USA TODAY, FEBRUARY 24, 2003

called restriction enzymes. They are also called molecular "scissors," because they can cut DNA at very specific points along the double helix. For instance, one enzyme might cut a strand of DNA in every spot that has the sequence ATCGTA. Scientists know about hundreds of restriction enzymes, and the list is still growing.

A TURNING POINT

This discovery was a turning point in the development of genetic engineering. Scientists use bacteria for these experiments because they are simple organisms. And they multiply quickly. Researchers can see the results of their work almost immediately. Then they can quickly produce large quantities of new substances. Scientists already knew that bacteria have small, circular pieces of DNA, called plasmids, floating freely within their cytoplasm. When restriction enzymes were discovered, scientists wondered if they could be used to cut and recombine different organisms at the molecular level. They hoped they could pick specific desirable traits from one organism and transfer them to another organism without getting unwanted characteristics.

Researchers found that after a gene had been isolated, they

could apply an enzyme called ligase—molecular glue—to splice the gene to another DNA fragment. This process would seal the plasmid with the new gene inside. After that, every time the bacteria reproduced, they would also reproduce the new gene contained in the plasmid. In 1973 Stanley Cohen of Stanford University and Herbert Boyer of the University of California in San Francisco successfully completed this procedure. They took a gene from a toad. Using restriction enzymes, they cut and pasted the gene into *E. coli* bacteria. *E. coli* bacteria are microscopic organisms that can be found in the human intestines. When these bacteria reproduced, the new gene was present. The "age of genetics" had begun. Cohen and Boyer called this technology recombinant DNA. It recombined two distinct strands of the double helix.

CLONING

Cloning is another technology that has evolved out of genetic research. While genetic engineering usually adds or removes just one or a few genes, cloning involves reproducing all the genes in an organism. Cloning means growing an exact copy of a plant or animal. Identical twins are natural clones. Identical twins have the same DNA because their mother's egg cell split into two parts shortly after it was fertilized. These two parts developed into two separate embryos that grew into two people.

In the 1950s and 1960s, scientists used various methods to clone frogs. Cloning mammals was much more challenging. Eventually, scientists learned to clone cows and sheep by splitting embryos. It became common for cattle ranchers to clone animals with desirable characteristics. In July 1996, Ian Wilmut of the Roslin Institute in Scotland took cloning one step further. He succeeded in cloning a sheep named Dolly with DNA taken from an adult sheep's cell. By the early twenty-first century, scientists were cloning dogs and cats.

Some researchers feel that cloning will make genetic

engineering more efficient. For instance, if researchers spent a long time developing a genetically engineered animal, cloning would allow them to make as many copies of the "new" animal as desired in a shorter amount of time. These processes are types of biotechnology. Biotechnology is the use of living organisms, such as yeast or bacteria, to serve human needs. Some traditional forms of biotechnology are bread making and beer making. These procedures use yeast to make products for human consumption. Cheese, vinegar, and wine are also products of this traditional science. Some scientists see genetic engineering as a natural extension of these older forms of biotechnology.

But this sophisticated technology raises many controversial issues. Because of its many applications, different fields of biotechnology have their own unique issues. The questions that arise from the development of new plants and animals are different from those related to human life or the environment. A careful consideration of each of these fields will enable people to think about how to use this technology for the progress of humankind and how to avoid its potential perils.

Below: Biotechnology has been used for thousands of years in human activities such as bread making. Adding yeast to the dough starts a biological process that raises the dough.

CHAPTER TWO

Transgenic Plants

In 2008 the world's population reached 6.7 billion. But by 2050, if the population continues to grow at its present rate, more than 11 billion people will be living on Earth. How will all these people be able to get enough food—especially those in newly developing countries? There, resources are already strained. And their populations are rapidly increasing. Some people think that if researchers can develop better plants through genetic engineering, then the food supply will be adequate for the increased population.

Why can't researchers develop superior new plants by using traditional methods? A technique called selective breeding (creating hybrids) has been used for many years. But it doesn't offer much promise of solving the immediate needs of the world's hungry people. By breeding the strongest, best-tasting, most nutritious plants and those most resistant to disease, growers have produced hardier crops. Selective breeding, however, takes time. Producing genetically engineered plants is faster.

Left: A youg woman dishes out lunch for a group of people in Haiti. In many developing countries, food resources are scarce. Some people hope genetic engineering of plants will help feed the world's growing population.

> ❝ **If we don't do this kind of work [genetic engineering of plants], the . . . [rich people] of the world will get along just fine. They can afford nutritious food. . . . The people of Cambodia and Africa can't, and won't be able to any time soon.** ❞
>
> —**CHARLES ARNTZEN,** DIRECTOR THE CORNELL- BASED BOYCE THOMPSON INSTITUTE FOR PLANT RESEARCH
>
> **USA TODAY** JUNE 7, 2000

Roger Beachy, a professor of biology at Washington University in Saint Louis, Missouri, said: "Traditional plant breeding approaches take between five and seven years . . . to produce a virus-resistant crop species. What we've been able to do by the new direct gene transfer [transgenic] approach is to produce disease resistance within nine to twelve months." Those who favor this method point out that genetic engineering can lead to larger crop yields with improved nutrition.

EDIBLE VACCINES?

There is even the promise of edible vaccines. In 2000 Charles J. Arntzen and other researchers at the Boyce Thompson

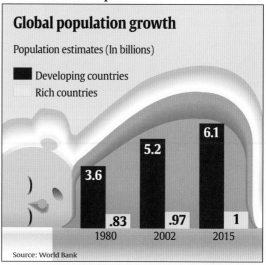

USA TODAY Snapshots®

Global population growth

Population estimates (In billions)

■ Developing countries
□ Rich countries

	1980	2002	2015
Developing countries	3.6	5.2	6.1
Rich countries	.83	.97	1

Source: World Bank

By Shannon Reilly and Frank Pompa, USA TODAY, 2004

Institute for Plant Research at Cornell University in Ithaca, New York, developed a type of genetically engineered potato. It contains protein from a virus that causes diarrhea. When they fed these genetically engineered potatoes to twenty human volunteers, nineteen out of the twenty developed resistance to the virus. Some researchers hope to introduce plants that could be used as edible vaccines into less developed countries. This might save millions of lives. And it would cost less than traditional vaccines. Researchers also pointed out that many people prefer eating a vaccine to being injected with one.

BUILT-IN DEFENSE SYSTEMS

Plants can also be genetically altered to have built-in defense systems against insect pests. This genetic technique could mean that fewer chemical pesticides would be used. Researchers at the Monsanto Company, for example, have spliced a gene from a natural soil bacterium called *Bacillus thuringiensis* (Bt) into potatoes. This microorganism has been used widely for years as a biopesticide—a naturally occurring insect killer. The biopesticide is considered harmless to humans and wildlife. Bt genes have also been successfully spliced into cotton, corn, and other crops often ravaged by insects. When an insect digests the genetically modified plants, a toxin—or poison—is produced within the gut of the insect, and it dies.

The Monsanto Company views this technology as one way to cut the enormous cost of insect damage to crops. It would also reduce the use of chemicals. According to *New Bio News*, a Monsanto Company publication, when harmful insects are killed by the Bt gene, beneficial insects will have an easier time controlling pests such as aphids.

Genetic engineering has also been used to develop plants with resistance to herbicides—chemical weed killers. When herbicides are sprayed to kill weeds, they can kill beneficial plants as well. Inserting genes that make plants immune to these chemicals can help farmers use their land more productively, proponents say.

BUILT-IN RISKS

Not everyone sees it this way, however. Hope Shand is the research director for Action Group on Erosion, Technology and Concentration (ETC Group). ETC deals with issues including agriculture and biotechnology. She urges caution as scientists embark on this new agricultural path. "While new biotechnologies do have potential to address food and agricultural problems in the developing world," Shand says, "it is critically important to look at the social, economic, as well as ecological risks associated with the introduction of these new technologies."

She questions whether the optimistic promises that some corporations have made regarding biocrops will ever occur. She questions the companies' motives too. "The bottom line," she says, "is that agrichemical corporations are not developing herbicide tolerant varieties because they want to clean up the environment, but because they are interested in selling more herbicides." She gives the example of genetically modified cotton. Calgene, a biotech company in Davis, California, developed the cotton. This plant can withstand a weed killer called bromoxynil, which has been linked to birth defects in wildlife. Shand remarks that for the first time, farmers can spray this herbicide in the vicinity of the cotton without ill effects on the plant. But in 2000, Calgene, which was bought by the Monsanto Company, made a business decision not to continue producing the genetically engineered cotton.

As the Biotechnology Working Group, a public interest organization, says in its report, *Biotechnology's Bitter Harvest*: "The market strategy is clear. Many chemical herbicides kill crops as well as weeds, thus their use is limited. But if farmers plant crops that tolerate particular herbicides, the market for these herbicides will increase."

One of the most controversial developments in high-tech agriculture was created by Delta and Pine Land, a seed company in Mississippi. Called genetic use restriction technologies, or GURTs, this genetic manipulation stops plants from producing seeds that can grow into new, healthy plants.

People who oppose GURTs call it terminator technology, or "suicide seeds." In 2006 almost five hundred organizations—including churches and farmers' organizations—joined in the Ban Terminator Campaign. The organization called upon the world's governments to stop the technology. In his book *Superpigs and Wondercorn*, Dr. Michael Fox, a veterinarian, urges scientists and the public to carefully evaluate the risks of high-tech agribusiness. He writes, "We are trying to improve conditions for ourselves too often at nature's expense; the environment is perceived as a resource, and all nonhuman life is inferior and thus expendable or exploitable without any ethical constraints."

Fox compares the present situation to the so-called Green Revolution of the 1960s. Developed nations brought high-tech farming methods to newly developing countries. He explains, "Agribusiness [industries involved with farming production, equipment, processing, and distribution] technology experts, super breeds of crops,

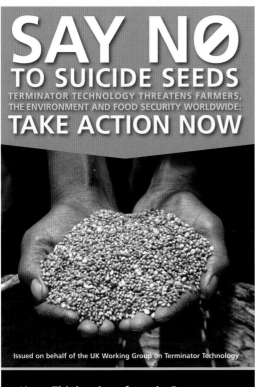

Issued on behalf of the UK Working Group on Terminator Technology

Above: This brochure from the Ban Terminator Campaign encourages people to reject suicide seeds, which are genetically altered to not be able to reproduce.

irrigation and hydroelectric dams, chemical fertilizers, pesticides and agripoisons exported to less developed countries produced great short-term profits but destroyed already existing, more regenerative, traditional farming practices, ultimately destroying the communities and the fragile land." In other words, Fox believes that experts encouraged farmers in many underdeveloped countries to stop growing traditional varieties of crops and to adopt new varieties. Some of these changes caused farmers to become dependent on pesticides and fertilizers. He stresses that 70 percent of the food sources come from "agrichemical fields" that produce only a few basic food crops. When there is more biological diversity, he maintains, the ecosystem is stronger.

In contrast, some scientists think that Earth's resources are so strained that there is no time to waste. They see genetic engineering as the greatest hope for improving agriculture. They want to use this technology immediately. Fred

Davison, former president of the University of Georgia, remarks that future plants that are drought resistant produce their own pesticides. Such plants can even be irrigated with salt water in areas near oceans. That could help farmers expand their markets. Davison says, "We're on the edge of a brand-new day. It's a little frightening to some of us, but the fact is, we're there, and our very survival depends on it."

Are critics of the genetic approach to agriculture suggesting that we take a step backward and reject the new technology entirely? Not necessarily. Fox thinks that this new science has its place in the modern world if used properly and with adequate caution. He feels that genetically engineered crops that are drought- and salt-resistant are beneficial and appropriate applications of biotechnology.

BRAVE NEW FOODS

In addition to environmental and economic concerns, transgenic plants also bring up the question of food safety. Are these altered products radically different from traditional foods? Or are they simply a novel mixture of natural components in a new edible package? The introduction of "foreign" genes into food crops has caused a wide range of reactions from developers, consumers, and those in the food service industries. The National Wildlife Federation published the following "Biotech Menu":

Appetizer
Spiced Potato with Wax Moth Gene
Juice of Tomatoes with Flounder Gene

Entrée
Blackened Catfish with Trout Gene
Pork Chops with Human Gene
Scalloped Potatoes with Chicken Gene
Corn Bread with Firefly Gene

Dessert
Rice Pudding with Pea Gene

Beverage
Milk with Genetically Engineered Bovine Growth Hormone

Although this mock menu was created to make a point about unusual combinations of genes, every biofood on this list has actually been developed. Some are already on the market. Are these scientific creations "Frankenfoods," as some critics call them in reference to Frankenstein's scientific monster? Or are they reasonable attempts to increase and improve the food supply? Proponents of the technology argue that since all DNA—whether from a plant or an animal—contains the same basic chemicals, the unlikely blend of plants and animals is not so odd.

In May 1994, the U.S. Food and Drug Administration (FDA) approved the first transgenic food plant. The Flavr Savr tomato was the result of millions of dollars of research and development. The tomato was

Above: These Flavr Savr tomatoes were for sale at a grocery store. The introduction of genetically modified foods into the marketplace in the United States makes some people nervous.

developed when Calgene patented a process that removes the gene that causes tomatoes to become soft and then reinserts it backward into the plant. This "antisense" gene cancels out the gene for rotting. It was meant to allow the tomato to be picked from the vine when it is ripe and still make the long journey from farm to market to dinner table without bruising or rotting. (Usually tomatoes must be picked before they are ripe. That means the consumer sometimes gets a hard, tasteless fruit.)

Food producers and the FDA were convinced that the genetically treated tomatoes were safe. But some consumer and environmental groups were not convinced. The disagreement ended in 1997. Production of the genetically engineered tomatoes stopped because they turned out to be difficult to transport. In the early twenty-first century, transgenic foods in U.S. supermarkets can be found in the produce department. And they are commonly found in cereals, vegetable oil, rice and wheat products, and in some baby foods.

One of the potential risks of these recombinant foods, say critics, is the possibility that they might cause allergic reactions. If an allergic individual ate a biofood that had genes from an allergen spliced into it, would that person develop a reaction? No one knows for sure, because there are few ways to test for allergenicity.

Dr. Jane Rissler of the Union of Concerned Scientists worries that "maybe there are a few thousand people who are allergic to bananas. Now suppose a banana [gene] is put into broccoli. People who are allergic to bananas will not know to avoid eating broccoli." Critics worry about other issues as well. The Council for Responsible Genetics observes that genetically modified foods could exhibit "counterfeit freshness." Fruits and vegetables might continue to look fresh and nutritious, even when they are past their prime.

Opponents of these genetic technologies worry that people shopping at supermarkets might not realize that they are buying foods that are not nutritious or could even harm them. But those in favor of genetically engineering foods think this will increase our food supply.

RELIGIOUS AND ECONOMIC QUESTIONS

Some of the most complicated issues concerning transgenic foods involve ethics and religion. What if members of religious faiths with dietary laws, such as Judaism or Islam, eat biofoods that have genes from foods that are forbidden? Would these people be violating their religious laws? If vegetarians eat plants that contain animal genes, would they still be observing a diet that excludes meat?

Professor Joe M. Regenstein works at the Department of Food Science at Cornell University. He is also the head of the Cornell Kosher and Halal Food Initiative. He said that Jewish people who follow kosher dietary laws have no problem with eating foods with genes that have been genetically engineered into bacteria or into plants. However, he added, the question of genes from pigs, which are considered nonkosher (forbidden), into animals is still being debated. Regenstein says, "The question of . . . nonkosher genes, e.g. pig, into animals remains unresolved."

Muslims (people who practice Islam) are not allowed to eat pork. Foods that are allowed by Muslim dietary laws are called halal. Pork is not one of these allowed foods. Professor Regenstein comments, "For the Muslim community, the use of genes from *halal* animals into plants and bacteria is fine." In other words, Muslims may eat food that contains genes from animals engineered into plants and bacteria, as long as the genes come from animals that are allowed as food by Islamic law. "The final decision about a porcine [pig] gene into plants and bacteria has not been made, but seems to be moving towards rejection. The question of whether a synthetic gene made totally *halal* that happens

to have the same sequence as a porcine gene placed into plants or bacteria also has not been resolved, but there is some likelihood that it will be accepted."

Another issue is the possibility of genes spreading from genetically altered plants to wild relatives. If pollen were to spread herbicide resistance from gene-spliced plants to weeds, could it lead to the creation of super-weeds? Genes have already accidentally spread from genetically manipulated plants to farms where the owners have not chosen to grow genetically modified organisms (GMOs.) In 1998 two varieties of transgenic papayas were first planted in Hawaii. These plants were engineered to resist a disease called ring spot virus. But the GMO papaya crop was hit hard by a type of fungus. As a result, half of Hawaii's small papaya farmers have gone out of business.

In 2002 a GMO testing service called Genetic ID tested papaya trees in Hawaii. It concluded that genetic contamination was in 50 percent of the traditional varieties of papaya on Hawaii's

In that same year, the Kona Coffee Council, a group of coffee growers in Kona, on Hawaii's Big Island, together with four farmers' groups, wrote a resolution. It called for a ban on planting GMO coffee trees developed by the University of Hawaii. The coffee council and other groups feared that if GMO coffee trees were planted, they could spread genes to traditional varieties. Kona coffee is exported to places such as Japan, which is not in favor of genetically engineered foods. If genes from GMOs got into their organic coffee, the coffee growers could lose a large part of their market.

Above: A farmer in Hawaii checks on one of his genetically engineered papaya trees.

Big Island. In other words, genes from the genetically modified papayas were showing up in regular varieties.

> **There is the very real possibility that this technology [transgenics] could create mistakes that are . . . irretrievable [impossible to stop]. Some could be disastrous.**
>
> **—HUNTER LOVINS,** COFOUNDER OF THE ROCKY MOUNTAIN INSTITUTE, A COLORADO-BASED NONPROFIT RESOURCE POLICY CONSULTING GROUP
>
> USA TODAY JUNE 7, 2000

www.usatoday.com

USA TODAY

Life

SECTION D

April 24, 2003

Biotech traces found in regular corn

From the Pages of

USA TODAY

The U.S. Environmental Protection Agency (EPA) announced Wednesday that it has concluded an investigation into a case of contaminated corn that is small in scale but could indicate big problems in the regulation of biotech farming.

The EPA required seed corn producer Pioneer Hi-Bred International to test regular corn grown near genetically engineered corn on one of the company's experimental plots in Hawaii. No contamination was found from transgenic plants on the EPA-regulated plot, so the EPA is satisfied.

However, 12 of the plants had been pollinated by transgenic corn from a different test field and tested positive for biotech genes.

In a complicated twist, the investigation now shifts to the U.S. Department of Agriculture [USDA] because the contamination came from a plot that, although close by, is in USDA territory because it has fewer than 10 acres [4 hectares].

There are two possible ways the contamination could have occurred. Either Pioneer didn't follow the regulations, which it says it did to the letter; or the regulations weren't enough to prevent transgenic pollen from contaminating other plants.

This has serious implications because food-safety activists have expressed doubts that the government can effectively regulate the production of genetically engineered plants and animals. . . .

—Elizabeth Weise

Above: A worker at a Kona coffee belt farm in Hawaii demonstrates coffee picking. Kona farmers banned the planting of genetically modified plants to preserve the plants across the Big Island.

In November 2001, the scientific journal *Nature* published an article by Ignacio Chapela and David Quint. They are researchers from the University of California at Berkeley. The article explained that traditional varieties of corn in Mexico had been polluted by genetically engineered corn. Three months later, more than one hundred organizations signed a Joint Statement on the Mexican GM Maize [corn] Scandal. They urged action to prevent future genetic pollution.

Ronnie Cummins of the Organic Consumers Association comments that "after ten years of commercialization, this hazardous and unregulated technology is still spreading around the globe. However, consumers and farmers worldwide have continued to organize and slow down the speed of [spreading] genetically engineered crops."

CHAPTER THREE

Transgenic Animals

Experimental animals into which scientists insert human genes produce human body substances. This type of genetic engineering of animals is sometimes referred to as pharming, or molecular farming. At the Institute of Animal Physiology and Genetics Research in the United Kingdom, for example, scientists have spliced into sheep the gene that codes (gives instructions to cells) for the production of a human blood-clotting agent. This agent is valuable because it is in short supply. A person born without the blood-clotting agent can bleed to death. This genetically engineered substance is easy to harvest (collect) because it is produced in the sheep's milk.

Early in 2009, scientists with the FDA approved the first anticlotting drug to be produced by goats that have been given a human gene. Meanwhile, the FDA also approved the goats used to make the drug. According to an article in the *New York Times* by Andrew Pollack, this was the first time such animals were cleared under agency guidelines. The drug prevents fatal blood clots in people with a rare

Left: These transgenic sheep were genetically modified to produce AAT, a protein used to treat emphysema, a lung disease, in humans.

medical condition. The drug is a human protein (antithrombin) extracted from the milk of genetically engineered goats. GTC Biotherapeutics produced the anticlotting protein in a herd of two hundred bioengineered goats in central Massachusetts. The advantage of deriving the drug from goats, according to Thomas Newberry, a spokesperson for GTC, is that "if you need more, you breed more."

Genetically engineered animals may aid researchers in finding cures for other human diseases. For example, scientists have engineered pigs that produce human insulin. This hormone is needed by diabetics. Scientists have also engineered sheep that generate human growth hormone in their blood. Researchers at Pharmaceutical Proteins, Ltd., in the United Kingdom, have created genetically modified sheep. The sheep contain the gene that codes for AAT, a protein used in the treatment of emphysema, a lung disease. Before genetic engineering, only small amounts of the human blood-clotting agent and AAT were available. That's because the human body produces only small quantities of those substances.

A Dutch biotechnology company called Pharming has developed transgenic rabbits that produce a human protein in their milk. The engineered substance can be used to treat angioedema. This rare hereditary illness causes soft tissues to swell, causing pain—or sometimes death.

PLAYING GOD OR SCIENTIFIC PROGRESS?

An ongoing debate centers on whether scientists have the right to alter the genetic structure of living creatures—perhaps changing the course of evolution. (Evolution is the gradual process of change that takes place as plants and animals develop.) Proponents call it improving on nature. Opponents dub it playing God.

Jeremy Rifkin, author and activist, says in his book *Algeny* that when living things are viewed as mere bits of information, it's easy to lose sight of the sanctity of life. It is easier for people to accept the idea of genetically engineering an information system than it is of genetically altering a living animal.

Proponents of genetic engineering believe that if animals are well cared for, it is ethically sound to produce drugs in their milk or blood that can save human lives. Substances such as tissue plasminogen activator, tPA, (which dissolves blood clots in human heart attack victims) are extremely expensive to produce in large quantities in laboratories. Using transgenic animals to produce tPA, however, could provide great amounts of this lifesaving drug at a fraction of the cost.

Researchers are also experimenting with transgenic animals as potential organ donors for human patients. Called *xenotransplantation*, this word is derived from the Greek word *xenos*, meaning "foreign." In 1997 Robert Pennington desperately needed a new liver, but no human livers were available. Instead, his doctors attached Pennington to a transgenic pig's liver, outside of his body,

hoping it would filter his blood and keep him alive. The pig's liver came from a company called Nextran, which genetically engineered pigs to carry human genes. Pennington's doctors hooked him up to the pig's liver for seven days. Then a human liver became available and was transplanted into the man's body. The pig's liver had helped Pennington survive until a human liver was located.

In 2008 almost fourteen thousand organ transplants were performed in the United States, according to the Organ Procurement and Transplantation Network in Richmond, Virginia. In that same year, approximately ninety-nine thousand patients in the United States were still waiting for human organs for transplantation. Could modified animal organs save these people's lives?

Critics such as the Campaign for Responsible Transplantation (CRT) argue that "xenotransplantation poses a grave danger to human health because of the risk of transferring deadly animal viruses to the human

www.usatoday.com

USA TODAY

Life

SECTION D

September 23, 2002

The Farmer in the Lab; Consumers Wary of Biotech Animals

From the Pages of
USA TODAY

Catfish don't have their own hospitals, but when scientists gave some of them a moth gene, they started making an anti-bacterial protein to protect themselves from disease. . . .

The goals are often worthy: Alter the genetic composition of animals in a way that produces the world's food more abundantly; use animals as factories for human pharmaceuticals; change creatures so they are friendlier to the environment.

But are these useful animals or monsters? Do they pose a threat to the environment? Is it humane to create them? How should they be regulated? Is their meat and milk safe to ingest? . . .

The coming years will see a simple visit to the store becoming much more complex than "Paper or plastic?" as we are faced with transgenic meat that's lower in fat, milk that's more heart-healthy produced by cows containing rat genes, or an arthritis drug produced not in a factory but in [carefully purified] pig semen. . . .

As the science has sped up, industry hasn't been far behind. Already there are hundreds of transgenic and cloned animals around the country in labs and some farms.

—Elizabeth Weise

population." CRT points out that more than twenty-five diseases can spread from pigs to humans. And there could be porcine viruses that haven't yet been discovered. In addition, CRT contends that animal-to-human transplantation costs more than transplanting human organs into people.

Critics also say this animal-organ donor plan exploits animals. They argue that it causes needless suffering to animals, which are living, feeling beings. As Vernon Jennings of SustainAbility, an environmental consulting company in London, points out, "The real question is whether the purpose of nonhuman life is purely to satisfy the 'needs' of human beings."

FAST FOOD?

One potential promise of genetic engineering is its ability to speed up food production. Some proponents of new genetic technologies say that if animals could be altered to grow faster, then they could get to market quickly. That would provide more food for the world's ever-growing population. In September 2008, the FDA asked for public comments about genetically engineered animals that would be used as food for humans. The FDA said that meat producers would have to show that the food products are safe to eat before they could be sold. On January 15, 2009, the FDA set strict guidelines for regulating such animals. But products containing them will not require labeling. That same month, the FDA stated that the agency considers meat and milk from healthy cloned animals as safe for humans to eat and drink. Such food products are not expected to be available in supermarkets for several years. Yet regulation of the U.S. food supply is so haphazard and underfunded that many critics worry that federal agencies cannot adequately ensure the safety of genetically engineered foods—plant or animal—for human consumption.

For example, more than thirty kinds of genetically engineered fish are being developed. One company, Aqua Bounty Technologies in Waltham, Massachusetts, has genetically modified salmon to grow twice as fast as regular farmed salmon. The growing cycle for these fish requires less time. Consequently, less food has to be fed to the fish. In addition, the company believes that the quicker growth leads to reduced waste products. That reduction causes less impact on the environment.

Some critics worry that if transgenic fish accidentally escape into the wild, they might mate with wild fish. If this happens, critics contend, it could lead to the demise of some wild fish species. According to a study by two biologists at Purdue University in Indiana, if altered fish escape, they could conceivably wipe out entire native populations of fish.

Scientists Richard Howard and William Muir conducted experiments on live fish. They also used computer mod-

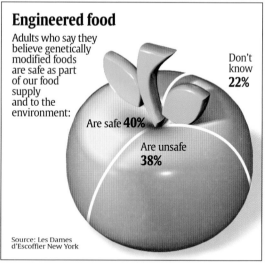

USA TODAY Snapshots®

Engineered food

Adults who say they believe genetically modified foods are safe as part of our food supply and to the environment:

Don't know **22%**

Are safe **40%**

Are unsafe **38%**

Source: Les Dames d'Escoffier New York

By Cindy Hall and Quin Tian, USA TODAY, 2000

els to predict future possibilities. The scientists demonstrated that sixty transgenic fish carrying growth hormones could lead to the possible extinction of sixty thousand healthy wild fish in forty generations. They said that even one fish could cause the same extinction, but it would take a longer time. Muir and Howard's study used fish called Japanese medaka. The medaka had had part of a salmon growth hormone gene inserted into their DNA.

Aqua Bounty thinks that its salmon do not pose a threat to the environment. Its transgenic fish are neutered (unable to breed). The company says that even if the fish managed to escape, they could not breed with native populations.

PIGS FOR A CLEAN ENVIRONMENT?

One problem with intensive pork production is too much phosphorus in the soil. Pig manure has a high concentration of phosphorus. This substance can build up in soil. Eventually, during heavy rains, runoff from farms can bring high amounts of phosphorus to local ponds and streams. The phosphorus pollutes the water. That leads to less oxygen in the water. This reduction, in turn, can kill fish and other aquatic life.

Some farmers feed their pigs an enzyme that helps the animals digest the phosphorus. Less phosphorus is excreted in pig manure. However, some people consider this approach too expensive.

Scientists at the University of Guelph in Ontario, Canada, believe they have a solution to this environmental problem. Cecil W. Forsberg and John P. Phillips of the Department of Molecular and Cell Biology have developed the Enviropig. The Enviropig is a transgenic animal that produces smaller amounts of phosphorus in its manure. The scientists' tests revealed that the GE pigs are healthy. And they excreted 60 percent less phosphorus than nonengineered pigs.

THE BUZZ ABOUT "LETHAL GENES"

Scientists from the University of California in Riverside and the U.S. Department of Agriculture are trying to save cotton crops from an insect pest called the pink bollworm. The tiny creature destroys $32 million worth of cotton crops each year. The insect starts life as a pink caterpillar. It bores its way into cotton plants, where it eats the seeds. After plumping up on its cottonseed meal, the caterpillar emerges as a tiny brown moth. The cycle continues when the mother lays eggs on cotton plants.

Pesticides have been used in many attempts to destroy the pink bollworm. And genetically engineered cotton plants that are meant to resist the pest have been developed. Still, the bollworm's devastation persists. In response to this challenge, UC–Riverside and the USDA's scientists took a "lethal gene" from a fruit fly. They programmed the gene to lead to the death of the next generation of fruit flies by interfering with the larva's development. To get the lethal gene into the pink bollworm's DNA, researchers first spliced the fruit fly gene into a "jumping gene." Jumping genes are stretches of DNA that can move from one location to another on the same chromosome. They can even move from one chromosome to another. Then the researchers used the jumping gene as a vector, or delivery system. The vector inserts the lethal gene into the pink bollworm's DNA. Researchers hope this will lead to their extinction.

Other insects are being genetically modified in the fight against human diseases. The World Health Organization estimates that between three hundred million and five hundred million people around the globe contract malaria each year. Between one million and three million people die of this disease annually. Malaria is caused by a microscopic parasite—a creature that lives off its host. This parasite lives inside a type of mosquito. When this type of mosquito bites a person, the parasites can enter the human bloodstream, where they multiply.

Scientists are trying to engineer mosquitoes with lethal genes. They hope that the GE mosquitoes will mate with malaria-carrying mosquitoes in the wild. Eventually, the experiment may lead to fewer malaria cases around the world. Scientists also hope that genetically modified honeybees will be able to survive diseases and fatal parasites that have destroyed many honeybees.

Opponents of these technologies point out that jumping genes could get out of control. Then they might leap into the DNA of beneficial insects such as praying mantises and ladybugs. What if engineered insects displayed unintended properties? Once out in the wild, some say, they might become bigger, more out-of-control pests.

Supporters of the technology think it is unlikely. They counter that a larger possibility is that the insects might not function as well in the wild as they do in the laboratory. Will these insects save the world from fatal diseases such as malaria and the destruction of crops? Or will they create bigger problems that can't be controlled? Only time will tell how these technologies will affect our world.

ANIMALS WITH HUMAN DISEASES

In 1988 researchers at Harvard University developed the Onco-Mouse. The OncoMouse is an animal genetically altered to carry an oncogene. The onco-gene makes the mouse prone to breast cancer. Funded by DuPont Company, researchers created the mouse to serve as a model for finding treatments for humans with the dreaded disease.

Shortly after the develop-ment of the OncoMouse, vet-erinarian Michael Fox called for a conference of religious leaders. Fox wanted to dis-cuss the implications of creat-ing this and other transgenic animals. Representatives from various religious denominations attended. Fox reported that con-ference attendees thought the public should voice its opinion too. Decisions about altering animals, they said, should not be left to scientists and corpo-rations alone. Technology, they said, affects everyone.

Since then scientists have engineered other animals to develop very high levels of cholesterol. The high cholesterol makes them prone to athero-sclerosis. The condition causes a loss of elasticity in the arter-ies, as well as coronary artery disease. Rheumatoid arthritis, a painful disease of the joints, and AIDS are other diseases that scientists hope to conquer by studying transgenic animal models. In 1987 Malcolm Martin and a team of researchers at the National Institutes of Health (NIH) in Maryland inserted the AIDS virus genome (all the genetic material of an organism) into mice. The mice then carried the virus in all their cells.

Some researchers hailed this as a breakthrough in the war against AIDS. But others wor-ried about what would happen if the animals escaped from the lab. If they mated with nor-mal mice, would their offspring carry the AIDS virus? And could this unleash a new, more severe epidemic of the disease in humans?

Dr. Robert Gallo codiscov-ered the AIDS virus. In 1990 he warned about the possibil-ity of the human AIDS virus combining with viruses that occur naturally in mice. This could potentially create new, deadlier "superAIDS" viruses. In addition, there is a question of whether those mice are even valid models for the human disease. In his book *The Human Body Shop*, Andrew Kimbrell says, "After several years of federally funded research . . . [the] AIDS mice were not only a new and unique potential danger in spreading AIDS, they also were capable of creating dangerous variations of the AIDS virus. Moreover, they were poor and potentially misleading research models for use in understanding the deadly disease." So if the AIDS virus could be changed by interacting with the mouse viruses, then any AIDS research done on these mice would be inaccurate.

What does the public think about engineering animals? In 2003 the Pew Initiative on Food and Biotechnology conducted a poll. The majority of Americans who participated in the poll (58 percent) oppose scientific research into the genetic alteration of animals. Of these, 46 percent said they were "strongly opposed."

People who are opposed point out that engineering animals can result in serious birth defects and cause animal suffering. Can we, however, ignore possible opportunities to improve human health? Some people think that research to save human lives is worth the cost in animal lives.

Critics insist that genetic engineering is not an exact science. They cite experiments by Dr. Ralph Brinster of the School of Veterinary Medicine at the University of Pennsylvania. In these experiments, mice were modified to carry the gene for human growth hormone. The mice grew to almost twice the normal size.

Scientists at the USDA research center in Beltsville, Maryland, engineered the same human gene into a pig. The resulting transgenic animal, however, was arthritic and cross-eyed. Andrew Kimbrell said that some people viewed the sickly pig as "the wretched product of a science without ethics."

GLOW-IN-THE-DARK ANIMALS

In addition to altering animals to produce human substances to use as models for studying diseases, scientists have also produced the first genetically modified pets. In 1999 researchers at the University of Singapore injected a gene from sea corals into zebra fish embryos. Normal zebra fish are black and silver. The researchers wanted to produce fish that would glow with a red light in the presence of certain pollutants so they could monitor water pollution.

However, the modified fish glowed all the time, so the original idea didn't work.

In 2003 a U.S. company decided to import the fish as novel pets. Critics worried that if the fish got loose, they could cause a threat to the environment. They also feared that this could be the beginning of many genetically engineered pets for sale. The Center for Technology Assessment and the Center for Food Safety went to court to prevent the sale of these GloFish. The lawsuit was dismissed in

Above: A GloFish swims in a pet store aquarium. Some people want to ban the fish in the United States because they fear negative consequences if it enters the natural environment.

> ❝ **GloFish's developers say the fish don't raise any environmental concerns because they can't survive in the wild.** ❞
>
> —**MICHAEL RODEMEYER,**
> **USA TODAY** DECEMBER 29, 2003

2005. Since then GloFish have been selling in the United States.

Fluorescent fish aren't the only modified animals that glow. In 2006 researchers at the National Taiwan University created three transgenic pigs that have a light green glow. Researchers at the university injected pig embryos with a gene from a jellyfish. Shinn-Chih Wu, a professor at the university, said that even the animals' hearts and inner organs are green. Professor Wu said he hopes these technologies

> ❝ **The National Academy of Sciences released a . . . report on the food safety and environmental issues raised by genetically engineered animals. . . . It found the biggest dangers were the potential for genetically engineered fish, shellfish and insects to escape into the wild and replace their natural cousins.** ❞
>
> —**MICHAEL RODEMEYER,**
> **USA TODAY** DECEMBER 29, 2003

Above: This transgenic pig glows green because genes from a jellyfish were inserted into its DNA.

be altered to glow, then scientists can tell if new drugs are effective in destroying the disease.

SILK FROM MILK

Genetic engineering can also be used to produce proteins other than human bodily substances. In 2002 Nexia Biotechnologies, a Canadian company, inserted a spider gene into goats. This caused the goats to produce spider silk protein in their milk. The protein is extracted from the goat milk. Then it is spun and stretched in special machines. The machines make the silk almost as strong as spider silk. Although spiders could theoretically be used to make their own silk, the company prefers goats because they make it in greater quantities. The goats are also less aggressive toward one another. When large quantities of spiders are put together in close quarters, they often fight and even devour one another.

will help scientists in the future when they want to treat diseased organs with stem cells. (Stem cells can grow into any type of cell in the body, such as heart cells, brain cells, or blood cells.) If these cells can be engineered to glow, then scientists can tell if the cells are helping the patient to heal. Or if diseased cells can

The company calls its product BioSteel, because it is stronger and lighter than steel. In the future, it may be used to manufacture superstrong fishing line, tennis racquet strings, bandages, ropes, or durable material for clothing. In 2006 Professor Randy Lewis of the University of Wyoming began using grants from the U.S. Air Force and U.S. Army to help develop Nexia's silk technology. It will be used to make products such as bulletproof clothing. Soon shoppers might go to clothing stores to buy shirts and jeans that could last for many years, thanks to the genes scientists have "borrowed" from spiders.

CRYING OVER SPLICED MILK?

Another, more controversial aspect of genetically engineered milk is the use of a hormone that increases milk production in cows. Cows injected with the substance produce about 10 percent more milk. The debate is so intense that people with different opinions even use different names for the recombinant drug. Those who support its use call it BST, rBST (r for "recombinant, or genetically engineered"), or

bovine somatotropin. Opponents call it BGH, rBGH, or bovine growth hormone.

Dairy cows naturally secrete a hormone that causes their bodies to produce milk. Scientists have taken the gene that codes for this substance and spliced it into bacteria. The bacteria then act as molecular "factories." They provide a nearly unlimited source of this hormone. Once the bacteria have produced the desired amount of the hormone, they are destroyed. Then the substance is harvested. It is sold to dairy farmers, who inject it into their cows.

In 1993 the U.S. Food and Drug Administration approved the Monsanto Company's recombinant product after reviewing it for safety. Advocates applauded this decision. They said it would increase dairy cow efficiency. Advocates also praised the recombinant hormone. It could mean greater milk yields from fewer herds of cows. It might also lead to lower costs for animal feed and grazing land. Indeed, greater milk yields have been proved. But consumers still tended to reject milk produced with rBST. Dean Foods, the nation's largest dairy processor, no longer processes milk from rBST-treated cows. By 2008 grocery retailers Costco, Kroger, Wal-Mart, and Sam's Club stopped carrying such milk. The Starbucks Coffee Company and Chipotle Mexican Grill also announced that they will use only rBST-free dairy products.

In the twenty-first century, critics of the growth hormone remain concerned about human health, animal welfare, and future economic and environmental repercussions. One concern is about IGF-1, or insulin-like growth factor-1. In separate letters to the FDA and to the attorney general of Maine, Michael Hansen, senior scientist at New York-based Consumers Union, warned of a potential link between IGF-1 and cancer. He cited studies showing an increase in IGF-1 in the milk of cows treated with BST/BGH. He added that studies suggest that IGF-1 can survive human digestion and be absorbed by the body.

Hansen concludes: "There are still unanswered questions [about the engineered hormone]. Increasing evidence shows that IGF-1 is clearly linked to cancer, especially breast, colorectal, and prostate cancers. Recent studies show that increased dairy consumption in women leads to increased serum IGF-1 levels." Another study, carried out by the European Union's Scientific Committee on Veterinary Measures Relating to Public Health, said that milk from BST/BGH-treated cows may cause allergic reactions and even cancer.

One possible side effect of BST/BGH is mastitis, the inflammation of a cow's udder. To cure this condition, farmers must give antibiotics to sick cows. Some scientists worry that residues in milk will lead to consumers developing antibiotic resistance. If these people got sick, antibiotics might not cure them. Hansen presented testimony before the Veterinary Medicine Advisory Committee on Potential Animal and Human Health Effects of rBGH. He stated that in addition to data on increased mastitis, there is also disturbing data on somatic cell counts (SCC)—a measure of pus cells found in milk. "Milk from treated cows has a higher SCC," he explains. This means that milk from treated cows contains a greater amount of pus than milk from untreated cows.

The Monsanto Company was formerly a major producer of the recombinant drug. The company maintained that since federal and state regulations monitor the presence of antibiotic residues, milk and meat from cows injected with the hormone are safe for human consumption. The FDA agreed. And the *Journal of the American Medical Association* issued a statement that said "the FDA has answered all questions and concerns about the safety of milk from BST-supplemented cows."

What does the general public think about this issue? Before the FDA approved the drug, eleven studies examined consumers' opinions. The results show that consumers prefer to buy milk from cows that are not treated with the genetically engineered hormone. Yet the labeling issue seems to be the major fight. Consumer advocates want labeling, while agribusiness fights it.

In 2002 state activists in Oregon attempted to bring about local reform of GMO food labeling. Measure 27, an effort to give people a voice in statewide food labeling policies, was offered on the 2002 Oregon ballot. The question was simple: should the state of Oregon require labels for GMOs?

Consumers Union wrote a letter to the governor of Oregon supporting Measure 27. The organization claimed that many laws, at the federal, state, and even local level, are designed to inform consumers of facts they want to know about food. The organization argued that people want to know about the genetic makeup of their food. Therefore, state laws should require GMO labeling. But the measure failed.

Dennis Kucinich, a congressman from Ohio, believes that the lack of proper labeling misleads the average shopper. In

USA TODAY Snapshots®

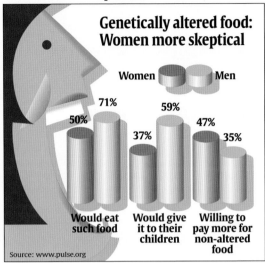

Genetically altered food: Women more skeptical

Women   Men

	Would eat such food	Would give it to their children	Willing to pay more for non-altered food
Women	71%	37%	47%
Men	50%	59%	35%

Source: www.pulse.org

By Lori Joseph, and Sam Ward, USA TODAY, 2000

2003 he introduced the Genetically Engineered Food Right to Know Act. He claimed that people want to know whether the food they purchase and consume contains genetically engineered material. The act would have required the FDA to mandate GMO labeling. The bill, however, did not pass.

And the FDA does not require special labels for products produced from cows given rBST, but consumers are demanding it. Demand for rBST-free milk has increased 500 percent since Monsanto introduced the hormone. Organic milk is the fastest-growing sector of the organic food market.

Many companies in the United States have refused to buy or sell milk from cows injected with the hormone. How have other countries reacted? The European Union and Canada have not approved the use of BGH/BST. In 2008 Monsanto sold its BGH/BST business to Ely Lilly & Company's animal division, Elanco. Some opponents of the transgenic hormones, including Andrew Kimbrell of the Center for Food Safety, an environmental organization, think the sale was due to consumer opposition to Monsanto's genetically engineered growth hormone.

CHAPTER FOUR

Engineering Humans

On September 14, 1990, a four-year-old girl named Ashanthi DeSilva became the first human to undergo a new form of therapy called gene therapy. The child lived with her family in the suburbs of Cleveland, Ohio. She suffered from an inherited disease called severe combined immune deficiency (SCID). People with SCID are born without a gene that codes for an enzyme called adenosine deaminase (ADA). The enzyme is important for the body's immune system. Without this enzyme, even the most common infections can be life threatening.

To help Ashanthi's immune system function more normally, her doctors prescribed a drug called PEG-ADA when she was two years old. The drug gave her the ADA enzyme that her body lacked and could not produce. The medicine also had some chemicals mixed in. They made it possible for the ADA enzyme to function in Ashanthi's body. This helped the young

Left: Ashanthi DeSilva, shown here in 1993, was the first human to undergo gene therapy.

girl survive. But it was not a permanent cure. The ADA enzyme helped for only a short time. It had to be replenished every few days. In addition, the treatment cost a great deal. And Ashanthi's doctors knew that this enzyme would not necessarily work well for every patient.

A more permanent solution was needed. In 1990, after obtaining permission from Ashanthi's parents and the National Institutes of Health, doctors took immune cells from Ashanthi's body. Dr. W. French Anderson and colleagues Drs. R. Michael Blaese and Kenneth Culver were working at the National Institutes of Health at the time. They genetically modified the cells to function as normal cells. The new cells then had to be put back into Ashanthi's body. The doctors chose viruses for this job, because they naturally invade cells. A virus is a microscopic organism that lives in the cells of other living things. By itself, a virus is a lifeless particle that cannot reproduce. But inside a living cell, a virus becomes an active organism. It

can multiply hundreds of times. As new viruses are produced, they are released from the cell and go on to invade other cells. The doctors used a virus that was genetically modified to remove its harmful genes to transport the corrected cells to Ashanthi.

Ashanthi's immune system initially responded well to the gene therapy. But the improvement in her condition is still not a final cure for her disability. She will continue to need additional treatments as the genetically altered cells need to be replaced. Still, she can hope to lead a more normal life as a result. In addition, she continues to take the PEG-ADA drug.

Anderson and his team were encouraged by the results of Ashanthi's gene therapy. The doctors performed the same type of gene therapy on another child, just four months later. Cindy Cutshall, who was nine years old at the time, also suffered from ADA deficiency. Like Ashanthi, she responded well to the therapy. She is also taking reduced dosages of the PEG-ADA drug and continues to do well.

GENETIC TRAGEDIES

Ashanthi and Cindy's stories ended on a happy note. Years later, however, another experiment in gene therapy ended in tragedy. In September 1999, Jesse Gelsinger, an eighteen-year-old man from Tucson, Arizona, enrolled in a gene therapy trial at the University of Pennsylvania. Jesse suffered from OTC, a rare liver deficiency. Jesse had inherited a broken gene that prevents the liver from producing an enzyme needed to break down ammonia. Poisonous levels of ammonia could have built up in his body. However, Jesse's condition was not life threatening. He controlled it by eating a low-protein diet and taking medications.

He agreed to be the recipient of gene therapy in the hopes that it could lead to therapies for children born with a more threatening form of the disease. The researchers told him they had performed the same experiment without severe side effects on animals and humans. But this time, they increased the dosage. The researchers put the needed gene into a type of virus that was made harmless. The scientists decided to directly inject the gene-carrying virus into the artery that led to Jesse's liver—even though some scientists thought this might be dangerous. Four days after the treatment, Jesse died. His kidneys, liver, lungs, and brain had failed. The cause may have been a severe reaction to the genetically engineered virus that was used to transport the new genes into Jesse's body.

After this tragedy, researchers did what they could to make sure that nothing like this would happen again. The FDA, together with the National Institutes of Health, investigated the University of Pennsylvania studies and other human gene therapy studies. The investigators found that Jesse had had high amounts of ammonia in his body at the time of the study. They concluded that the researchers should not have included him in the experiment. He had been too sick to be part of the clinical trial. Investigators also found that two patients in similar experiments experienced serious side effects. Monkeys who were given this type of treatment had died. But no one told this to Jesse Gelsinger or his family when they were asked to give their informed consent to the experiment. ("Informed consent" means a person going into an experiment understands what it is about, including all the risks, and has given consent to participate.)

rules require that researchers report any unexpected problems that result from their gene therapy studies. But only about thirty-five serious problems were reported out of almost one thousand experiments during the investigation. The investigation also found that at least six other unreported deaths resulted from gene therapy experiments.

Another tragedy occurred when Dr. Alain Fischer, at the

> " **Eighteen-year-old . . . [Jesse] Gelsinger died after receiving a highly experimental gene therapy at the University of Pennsylvania . . . critics say the researchers didn't fully understand the risks of that treatment before starting a human trial.** "
>
> **—KATHLEEN FACKELMANN**
> **USA TODAY** , NOVEMBER 26, 2002

The FDA and NIH investigation concluded further that some other gene therapy researchers were not reporting all the harmful effects that resulted from their experiments. Government

Necker Hospital in Paris, France, carried out gene therapy experiments on children with a severe form of SCID. In May 2001, he traveled to a meeting of the American Society of Gene

" **It's too easy to say, '... why haven't we cured all these diseases? But when you're pioneering a new field, there are going to be advances and setbacks that are going to frustrate both the scientists and the public.** "

—**DANIEL SALOMON,** QUOTED IN LIZ SZABO, "GENE THERAPY'S SLOW
PATH; WHAT STARTED AS A REVOLUTION HAS RUN INTO ROADBLOCKS"
USA TODAY APRIL 5, 2005

Therapy. There, he announced his success in treating young patients with the life-threatening disease. He had inserted normal copies of the gene into eleven patients. Ten of them had improved. But in later years, three of these patients developed leukemia, a type of cancer of the blood. The children were treated with chemotherapy to stop the cancer. But one of the patients eventually died of the disease.

In 2003 the FDA responded by halting twenty-seven gene therapy studies using the same type of virus until they could investigate further. Dr. Theodore Friedmann, president of the American Society of Gene Therapy, commented, "Gene therapy remains a highly regulated form of medicine. [This] serves to maximize the likelihood of clinical success, but it also has an effect on the pace ... [of testing.]" Friedmann thinks progress may slow down if studies are temporarily or permanently stopped. He added that when children died as a result of the gene therapy studies in France and U.S. research was halted, authorities in Britain chose to continue such studies. "[British authorities] ... saw more benefit than danger in a similar study there and did not halt or delay additional clinical work with that disease."

GENE THERAPY FOR THE FUTURE

Some scientists still think gene therapy is a promising field if they proceed carefully. Maurice Swanson, a professor at the University of Florida, and colleagues performed successful gene therapy experiments on mice. The animals had been genetically engineered to carry defective genes. The genes caused the animals to develop muscle problems. The problems were similar to those of human patients with muscular dystrophy—a group of diseases that bring about a gradual deterioration of muscles. The most common form of muscular dystrophy is myotonic dystrophy. When people with this disease tighten their muscles, it becomes very difficult for them to relax the muscles again. Eventually, the sufferer's muscles get weaker and weaker. Finally, the muscles waste away.

Swanson's experiments built on knowledge from previous research at the University of Florida and the University of Rochester School of Medicine and Dentistry. That research showed that defective genes cause myotonic dystrophy. Swanson and colleagues injected mice with normal copies of a gene inserted into disarmed viruses. Twenty-three weeks after the altered mice received these injections, the muscle problems were completely eliminated. This treatment may hold a future cure for humans with the disease. There have been some successes and some devastating failures. But gene therapy research continues. Friedmann commented, "There are few, if any, forms of major medical intervention that are free of risks and dangers, and gene therapy will not be an exception."

TINY BUBBLES

Scientists are pursuing other ways of delivering corrective genes into people with inherited flawed genes. Fischer's studies and the one that led to Jesse Gelsinger's death used viruses that had been made harmless to carry the genes into the patient's body. Instead of using viruses, researcher Paul Grayburn and colleagues from the Baylor University Medical Center in Texas experimented in 2006 with microscopic bubbles. They used the bubbles to deliver insulin genes. They hope this experiment might lead to a future cure for diabetes.

Diabetics do not produce sufficient insulin to properly break down glucose (a type of sugar) in the blood. Some diabetics do produce insulin. But their bodies don't respond to it normally. This situation results in high levels of glucose in the blood. This leads to extreme thirst, frequent urination, lack of energy, and other symptoms. If left untreated, the disease can be fatal.

Grayburn and his team inserted the human gene for insulin into plasmids. Then they put the gene-carrying DNA found in bacteria into special microbubbles. The bubbles have a special shell. It does not dissolve like regular bubbles in the presence of liquids. In 2006 the research team injected these bubbles into the pancreases of rats. (The pancreas secretes hormones such as insulin into the blood-stream.) Then the researchers used ultrasonic pulses directed toward each rat's pancreas. These pulses burst open the bubbles. Then the plasmids entered the rats' organs. The researchers later found high levels of human insulin in the rats. Someday the treatment may help those who suffer from diabetes.

Another possible genetic treatment uses a different method. In 2006 Professor Andrew Z. Fire of Stanford University and Professor Craig C. Mello of the University of Massachusetts Medical School shared a Nobel Prize in Physiology or Medicine for the discovery of RNA (ribonucleic acid) interference. RNA is a close cousin of DNA. Instead of inserting a gene, RNA interference (RNAi) seeks to turn off genes that may cause diseases or disable genes that invading viruses need to multiply. When genes are turned off, they do not produce certain proteins.

As of 2008, the FDA had not approved the sale of any human gene therapy product. Some scientists have high hopes that gene therapy might provide cures for inherited diseases such as cystic fibrosis (which causes large amounts of mucus to build up in a sufferer's lungs) and hemophilia (a condition that can cause a person to bleed to death). Others urge caution until we know more about its long-term effects.

A MAP OF HUMANITY: THE HUMAN GENOME PROJECT

To learn more about the mysteries of human DNA, the Department of Energy and the National Institutes of Health coordinated the Human Genome Project (HGP). The project launched in 1989. Other countries, including the United Kingdom, France, Denmark, Germany, and Italy, had similar programs. The project's goals included mapping (locating and identifying) where genes lie on the chromosomes within a cell and then sequencing genes—discovering the order of the As, Ts, Cs, and Gs within all the different genes.

On June 26, 2000, then president Bill Clinton announced that the international HGP and Celera Genomics Corporation had both completed a "working draft" sequence of the human genome. (The draft sequence covered

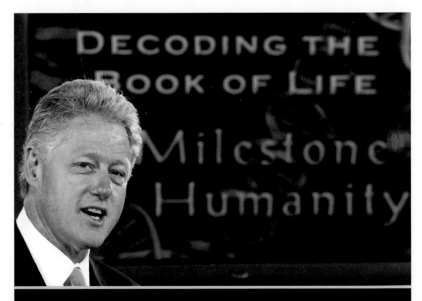

Above: President Bill Clinton announces the completion of a working draft sequence of the human genome on June 26, 2000.

about 90 percent of the genome.) In April 2003, fifty years after Watson and Crick discovered the structure of the DNA molecule, the Human Genome Project had completed rough drafts for each human chromosome. But more details were needed. In May 2006, Human Genome Project researchers finally announced their completion of DNA sequences for all human chromosomes. The data is freely available to scientists and the public on databases on the Internet.

The project has been applauded by many who expect it to revolutionize medicine. In the future, genetic predispositions might be discovered at birth or even before. Researchers anticipate that most medicine will become preventive rather than curative. Diseases might be prevented genetically rather than cured by prescriptions or procedures.

Gene testing is becoming a more and more common practice. A person can even purchase a kit on the Internet, spit into a tube, and send it back to the lab from which it came. Certified lab technicians analyze the DNA and send results in a few weeks. An Internet connection to the lab helps interpret the results. The lab even offers online discussion groups.

TROUBLING PREDICTIONS

Genetic testing can determine whether people carry defective genes even before the disease develops. But should people be told in advance that they have a gene for an incurable disease? In a 2004 interview with National Public Radio (NPR), Lauren Dubin of Olney, Maryland, explained how her life was changed dramatically by the current advances in genetic testing.

Dubin's mother, sister, and cousins had all been diagnosed with breast cancer. She was afraid that this was more than just a coincidence. Dubin made an appointment with a genetic counselor to discuss her family's medical history. The clinic ran a series of tests. The tests showed that Dubin's family carried a particular gene known to cause breast cancer. According to the doctor, a high chance existed that Dubin would also develop the cancer. In her NPR interview on *All Things Considered*, Dubin says that this information gave her a sense of control that most women don't have. Because she knew about her genetic history, Dubin was emotionally prepared for breast cancer well before she was diagnosed with it.

The April 2, 2009, issue of the *New England Journal of Medicine* published the results of an eight-year study of 130,000 women in India. A new DNA test for human papillomavirus (HPV), the virus that causes cervical cancer, has proved more effective than the Pap smear or other methods used to detect early signs of the disease. Dr. Mark Schiffman of the National Cancer Institute thought that the implications of the findings of this trial were immediate and global. During a Pap smear, named for its inventor, Dr. George Papanicolaou, cells are scraped from the cervix. The cells are sent to a laboratory. There, a pathologist stains the cells and inspects them under a microscope to find abnormalities. Results usually take several days. The DNA screening also requires a cervical scraping. The cells are then mixed with reagents and read by a machine.

In most developing countries, Pap smears fail because there are too few pathologists. Also, women who are told to return to a clinic for results often cannot do so. The DNA test can run on batteries without

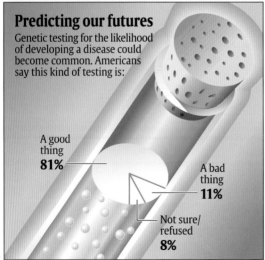

USA TODAY Snapshots®

Predicting our futures

Genetic testing for the likelihood of developing a disease could become common. Americans say this kind of testing is:

A good thing
81%

A bad thing
11%

Not sure/ refused
8%

Source: Harris Interactive   By Beth Liu and Frank Pompa, USA TODAY, 2003

water or refrigeration. It takes less than three hours and costs only about five dollars. The Indian study began in 1999. The study involved 131,746 healthy women ages thirty to fifty-nine from 497 rural villages. None of the women who were diagnosed negative on their DNA test died of cervical cancer. Pap tests, while helpful, are not as accurate because early signs of the cancer can go undetected.

However, some scientists question whether genetic testing is reliable—even though proponents trust the accuracy of such tests. In its "Position Paper on the Human Genome Initiative," the Council for Responsible Genetics states: "The assumption that genes (the genome) are the 'blueprint' of the organism and 'control' the way the organism develops and functions" is a "reductionist view, an oversimplification." Although genes are significant, "their structures and functions are affected by what goes on around them."

The report says that many genes contribute to human traits. It is impossible to predict how a defective gene will influence a specific individual. Knowing that an individual carries the gene for cancer, sickle cell anemia, or Huntington's disease, for example, does not explain when or how seriously a person will contract that disease. In addition, the discovery of a gene that causes a disease does not automatically guarantee that a cure will be found. The report states that "even if we knew everything... about the human genome, we would know only a tiny piece of the story." So genes alone do not give people their complex set of characteristics. Other factors shape a person's physical and mental traits. Environment, for example, can affect a person's health. So can the food a person eats. The report concludes, "The genome project vastly exaggerates the importance of genes."

DNA IN THE COURTS

Each individual's complete sequence of three billion base pairs—the order of their As, Cs, Ts, and Gs—is unique. That is why the DNA in blood, hair, or other bodily substances found at the scene of a crime can be compared to that of a suspected criminal. Sir Alec Jeffreys and others at the University of Leicester in Britain developed DNA testing in 1984. Such testing was originally used in paternity and immigration cases. The test could prove that parents and children were related. Jeffreys later established Cellmark Diagnostics, a DNA testing company in Britain and the United States.

DNA testing made court history in 1986. It was used to free an innocent man accused of rape and murder in Great Britain. In addition, DNA testing proved the guilt of the actual criminal. DNA testing is routinely used in court cases in the United States and in Europe.

DNA DATABANKS

On April 10, 1995, the world's first national DNA database was created in Great Britain. The

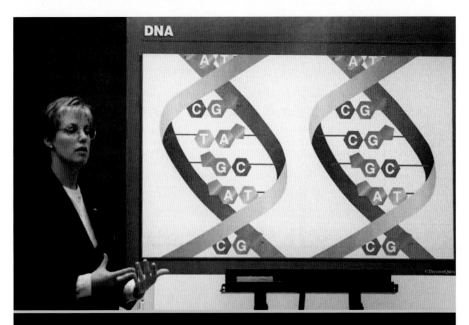

Above: A scientist explains DNA testing presented as evidence during the 1995 murder trial of U.S. football star O. J. Simpson.

database resulted from the controversial Criminal Justice and Public Order Act. The legislation gave police more authority to obtain hair and saliva samples for DNA testing of crime suspects. The American Civil Liberties Union (ACLU) issued a statement that says, "State and federal DNA databanks are expanding at an alarming rate." Although these databanks were at first created to track down dangerous criminals, the ACLU says that "police departments and [others] across the country have begun collecting and permanently storing DNA from arrestees and other innocent persons."

On April 24, 2008, then president George W. Bush signed into law the Newborn Screening Saves Lives Act. The purpose of the law is to set up a national plan to screen and store the DNA of all newborn babies in the United States. The bill states that the federal government should "continue to carry out, coordinate, and expand research in newborn screening"

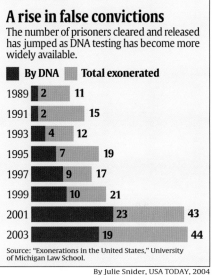

A rise in false convictions
The number of prisoners cleared and released has jumped as DNA testing has become more widely available.

■ **By DNA** ▨ **Total exonerated**

Year	By DNA	Total exonerated
1989	2	11
1991	2	15
1993	4	12
1995	7	19
1997	9	17
1999	10	21
2001	23	43
2003	19	44

Source: "Exonerations in the United States," University of Michigan Law School.

By Julie Snider, USA TODAY, 2004

and "maintain a central clearinghouse of current information on newborn screening ... ensuring that the clearinghouse is available on the Internet and is updated at least quarterly."

This law worries some groups such as the Citizens' Council on Health Care. In a report on its website, the council notes concern that the law will increase the use of genetic testing for children. It worries that personal information about infants and their families will be put into large national databases without their consent. The council also worries that

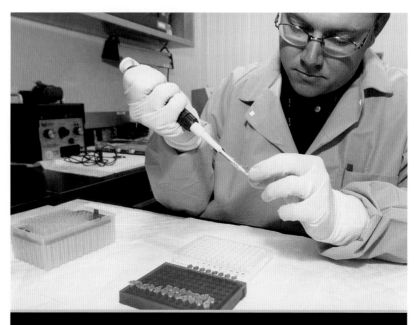

Above: A forensic scientist prepares a DNA sample from a crime scene at a lab in Richmond, Virginia. This sample will be tested against a national database to see if it matches DNA on file.

the list of "at risk" genes will grow. The report states: "As the list of trackable disorders and 'at risk' genes expands—perhaps to include obesity, diabetes, alcoholism, and violence—more children and families will be entered into genetic tracking registries for monitoring and assessment." Twila Brase, president of the council, said, "Soon, under this bill, the DNA of all citizens will be housed in government genomic biobanks and considered governmental property for government research." She strongly objects to the bill, saying that it strips "citizens of genetic privacy rights and DNA property rights."

Although each individual's DNA is unique, it is impossible to compare all of an individual's As, Ts, Cs, and Gs with samples of blood or bodily fluids. The samples are only a small portion of the total three billion bases that make up an individual's DNA. Forensic scientists look for special repeat patterns of As, Ts, Cs, and Gs that occur over and over again. These patterns vary from person to person. It is possible to find two or more individuals who have the same repeated pattern, but it is unlikely. For instance, one repeat pattern could show up twenty times in one person's DNA but only ten times in her sister's DNA. Scientists figure out the mathematical odds of a person's repeat patterns matching the sample found at a crime scene. If the odds are high, it is unlikely that the person tested is not guilty of the crime.

Although DNA evidence can land a suspect in prison, it has also helped to get wrongly accused people out of jail. Lawyers Barry C. Scheck and Peter J. Neufeld founded the Innocence Project in 1992. The nonprofit legal clinic is dedicated to representing prisoners who may have wrongfully been convicted of a crime. Many of these prisoners were in jail before DNA evidence was used. The Innocence Project requests samples of blood, hair, or other biological materials taken from the scene of the crime for which someone has been convicted. Then the DNA of the prisoner is compared to those samples. The Innocence Project inspired the founding of other institutions. Many of them are affiliated in a group called the Innocence Network. Altogether, as of December 2008, these organizations

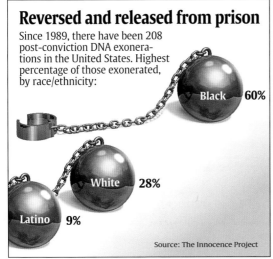

USA TODAY Snapshots®

Reversed and released from prison

Since 1989, there have been 208 post-conviction DNA exonerations in the United States. Highest percentage of those exonerated, by race/ethnicity:

Black 60%

White 28%

Latino 9%

Source: The Innocence Project

By David Stuckey and Karl Gelles, USA TODAY, 2007

July 10, 2008

DNA clears Ramsey family in JonBenet's death

From the Pages of
USA TODAY

The family of JonBenet Ramsey has been formally cleared of any role in the 6-year-old's 1996 slaying, a Colorado prosecutor announced Wednesday, citing newly discovered DNA evidence.

The Christmastime killing triggered a global news media frenzy and a controversial investigation that long focused on the child's parents, John and Patsy Ramsey, and JonBenet's brother, Burke.

Boulder, Colo[rado], District Attorney Mary Lacy said in a statement on Wednesday that DNA evidence recovered from the child's clothing pointed to an "unexplained third party." Lacy apologized to the family for the suspicions that made their lives "an ongoing living hell."

"The Boulder district attorney's office does not consider any member of the Ramsey family, including John, Patsy or Burke Ramsey, as suspects in this case," Lacy said in a public statement. "To the extent that this office has added to the distress suffered by the Ramsey family at any time or to any degree, I offer my deepest apology."

—Kevin Johnson

have proved the innocence of 225 prisoners and led to their being released from jail.

SOMATIC OR GERM-LINE MANIPULATION?

So far, most genetic manipulation has affected only individual patients, not their offspring. This type of manipulation is called somatic cell gene therapy. It affects all the body cells except the sex cells, also called germ cells. If researchers find ways to transform the germ cells, then gene transfers could be passed on to future generations. Therapy that affects a person's offspring is called germ-line gene therapy. It involves the insertion of new genes into the nucleus of sperm, eggs, or embryos. The new genes are then passed on from one generation to the next. This type of intervention could probably change the evolution of human life.

The Council for Responsible Genetics calls for a ban on germ-line manipulation. It says this therapy is not necessary to cure people. And they warn about its dangers. They comment that inserting foreign DNA into germ cells could have unpredictable repercussions. It could even lead to susceptibility to cancer and other fatal diseases. While proponents stress the health benefits for the human race, critics worry that germ-line therapy could be a genetic nightmare. We might see disease eliminated in the future. Or we could witness the creation of new and possibly more dangerous genetic conditions that cannot be cured once they are unleashed.

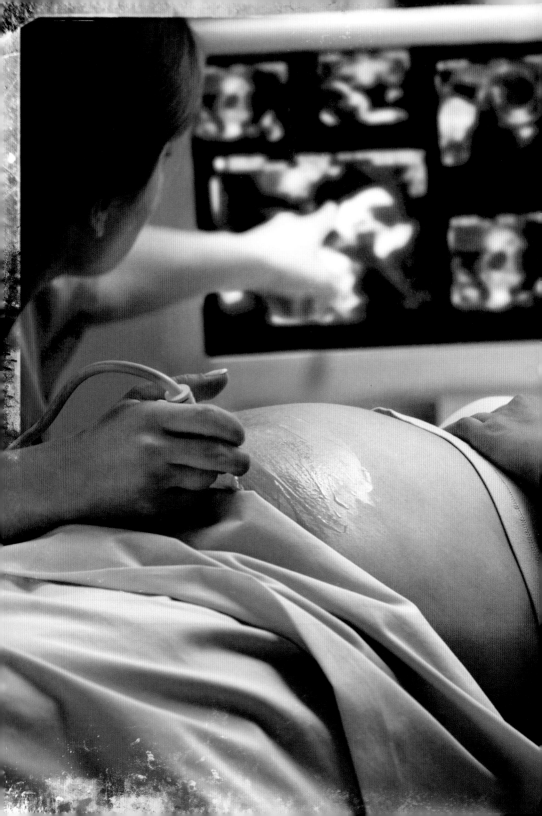

CHAPTER FIVE

The New Eugenics?

When discussing genetic engineering, the question of eugenics is often raised. Eugenics deals with improving hereditary qualities by controlling human mating. Eugenicists believe that the human race can be improved by deliberately encouraging people with "superior" traits to reproduce while discouraging people with "inferior" traits from bearing children. In 1883 Francis Galton coined the word *eugenics*. It comes from a Greek word meaning "wellborn."

In the United States, the Station for the Experimental Study of Evolution was established in Cold Spring Harbor in Long Island, New York, in 1904. Its mission was to train people for a few weeks and then send them to communities of poor people in New Jersey and New York. The researchers collected "data" on what they considered "hereditary" traits—such as "shiftlessness" and "feeblemindedness." This "science," with its stress on the supposed genetic component of inferior

Left: A doctor performs an ultrasound on a pregnant woman. Some people see genetic testing as the next step on the road to healthier children.

traits, led to involuntary sterilization laws (preventing people from bearing offspring). It also led to the U.S. Immigration Restriction Act of 1924. That law kept people from Asia and eastern Europe from coming to the United States. By 1931 sterilization laws were in effect in about thirty states. And twenty thousand Americans had been involuntarily sterilized. In California the sterilization law was not repealed until 1979. About nine states still had laws allowing forcible sterilization.

Dr. Ruth Hubbard of Harvard University is concerned about what she calls "the new eugenics." She says, "The idea of 'race purity' may have died; the idea of building a strain of supermen may have died; but the idea that it is more beneficial for certain people to have children than others, and that a vast range of human problems can be cured once we learn how to manipulate our genes, remains very much with us." Hubbard believes that this genetic approach places too much stress on the role of heredity. It also keeps people from addressing important health problems posed by environmental, social, political, and economic factors.

In a recent effort to fight global warming, government agencies in both the United States and Great Britain have promoted a policy of population control. Young couples, in their view, should have no more than two children. Jonathon Porritt, head of the Sustainable Development Commission in the United Kingdom, believes that "curbing population growth … must be at the heart of policies to fight global warming." He claims that "having more than two children is irresponsible" because of the negative effects booming population sizes have on the environment. Others see this as a policy of eugenics. The government, in their view, has no right to prevent families from having as many children as they want.

DESIGNER CHILDREN?

Are we headed toward a world where genetic technologies will allow people to choose what their children will look like? In the 1997 science fiction movie *Gattaca*, starring Uma Thurman and Ethan Hawke, parents picked their future children's attributes. Parents—if they had enough money—could leaf through catalogs to find the best-looking, most intelligent models. But designing children isn't just about giving your child the prettiest eyes and the most athletic frame. It can also be about saving lives. The 2004 TV documentary *Who's Afraid of Designer Babies?* tells the story of a couple who choose to have a team of doctors use preimplantation genetic diagnosis (PGD)—a technology for screening embryos—to ensure the survival of their unborn son.

The ability of parents to alter their child's genetic structure has caused serious controversy. In 2008 a storm of protests caused a Los Angeles clinic to cancel a program that allowed parents to choose their child's eye color. Protesters claimed that doctors should not tamper with the physical appearance of a child. According to them, nature should decide this. Despite criticism, a clinic in Southern California has

Below: In the movie *Gattaca*, Vincent Freeman, played by Ethan Hawke *(left)*, impersonates Jerome Morrow, played by Jude Law *(right)*. Morrow's genetic code was designed and Freeman's was not. In the movie, those with designer genes have a higher place in society.

scheduled the delivery of the first completely designed baby for 2010. The baby's gender, skin, hair, and eye color were all chosen by its parents.

Genetic testing can certainly be beneficial, however. Several tests diagnose birth defects after a woman has become pregnant. Ultrasound (high frequency sound waves) and amniocentesis are two of the most frequently used tests. With ultrasound, ultrasonic waves produce an image of the fetus (unborn child) on a computer screen. In amniocentesis, the doctor watches the position of the fetus while inserting a long, hollow needle through the mother's abdominal wall and into the uterus. The doctor withdraws some of the fluid surrounding the fetus. This liquid, called amniotic fluid, contains cells that can be used for genetic testing. With this procedure, doctors can accurately diagnose serious disorders, such as Down syndrome, that may affect the fetus.

Percutaneous umbilical blood sampling is another test. It uses blood from the umbilical cord rather than amniotic fluid. In chorionic villus sampling, doctors remove some of the tissue surrounding the fetus through a small tube inserted into the mother's vagina. The tissue is identical to that of the fetus. If the fetus has genetic defects, the doctor can tell the parents their options and provide counseling and emotional support to help parents cope.

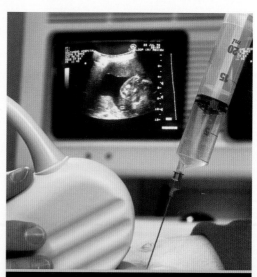

Above: A doctor is using this needle and ultrasound machine to perform an amniocentesis.

Preimplantaton genetic diagnosis tests embryos when a couple is at risk for passing on a gene for serious diseases such as cystic fibrosis. Doctors give a woman drugs so she will produce many eggs. The eggs are collected and fertilized in a dish with her husband's sperm. After a few days, the eggs grow to about eight cells. One or two cells are removed and tested for mutations. Doctors then select an embryo that does not carry the unwanted gene and implant it into the mother. There, it can continue to grow as in a normal pregnancy.

DILEMMAS OF DNA TESTING

Michelle Burruezo and her husband, Ryan Salinas, suspected something was wrong when their six-month-old daughter, Olivia Salinas, started to behave strangely. They took her to a local pediatrician. Seeing nothing abnormal, the doctor diagnosed Olivia with a mild ear infection and put her on antibiotics. Olivia did not improve. Her parents brought her to a regional hospital. There, doctors discovered that she had an abnormally enlarged heart. After running a series of tests, doctors discovered that Olivia had a rare illness known as Pompe disease.

Pompe disease was first discovered by Dutch doctor J. C. Pompe in 1932. The disease mutates a gene that allows the body to convert glycogen—a type of sugar—into energy. Because Pompe disease affects this gene, large amounts of glycogen build up in the body, especially around the heart. This causes the infant's heart to be abnormally large. Neither of Olivia's parents had the disease. But their DNA still carried the genes that cause it. By combining their DNA, they transmitted an active form of the disease to Olivia. Doctors said that she had less than two months to live.

But Olivia's parents did not give up. They contacted Barry J. Byrne, a Florida pediatrician who specializes in heart-related illnesses. Byrne had done research on Pompe disease. He made an important medical breakthrough in 2001. Byrne discovered that he could reduce the heart size of mice with Pompe disease by injecting them with a special enzyme. Months before Olivia's birth, the FDA allowed Byrne to conduct his experimental procedure on people. Olivia was one of the first patients to receive Byrne's treatment. Her story shows how people with rare genetic diseases can benefit from treatments developed from animal testing.

GENETIC DISCRIMINATION IN THE WORKPLACE?

Will employers and insurance companies avoid people who have genetic "flaws"? Will there be a new underclass of the "genetically challenged"—people who are considered inferior because of the "imperfect" genes with which they are born? The Americans with Disabilities Act (ADA) is a federal law passed by Congress in 1990. It forbids discrimination against people who are disabled. The Equal Employment Opportunity Commission (EEOC) is a U.S. government

Above: Observers in Washington, D.C., celebrate the passage of the Americans with Disabilities Act in 1990.

agency. It revised guidelines from March 15, 1995. The EEOC issued a statement that employers could not discriminate against otherwise healthy people who carry genes that might predispose them to genetic diseases. The EEOC stated that if people with these genes were perceived as disabled, then these cases would fall under the ADA's ban on discrimination.

In 2000 President Bill Clinton attempted to broaden protection against genetic discrimination. Clinton prohibited all federal departments from hiring or promoting anyone based on results from a genetic test.

In 2001 the EEOC took measures to protect employees from genetic discrimination. It settled the very first genetic discrimination lawsuit in U.S. history. In the suit, the EEOC brought charges against the Burlington Northern Sante Fe Railway (BNSF). The BNSF had genetically tested its employees for carpal tunnel syndrome, alcoholism,

> ❝ **In addition to federal protections, the majority of states have passed laws to protect individuals who undergo genetic testing. . . . Early detection, identification and treatment are often critical to success. In addition, as genetic-testing technology becomes more sophisticated, health professionals will need to know the results of genetic tests to avoid harmful medical errors.**
>
> —**HENRY DESMARAIS,** HEALTH INSURANCE ASSOCIATION OF AMERICA, "FEARS ARE OVERBLOWN,"
>
> ● USA TODAY AUGUST 20, 2002

and diabetes. The company did not tell their employees that the tests were genetic. Faced with discrimination charges, the BNSF settled the case with the EEOC and admitted its guilt.

In its 2001 paper "Genetic Discrimination," the Council for Responsible Genetics comments that "[genetic] discrimination [is] unjust, [and] it is scientifically inaccurate. Genes can tell us only part of the story about why some people get sick and others do not . . . because many genetic tests predict—with limited accuracy—that a disease may [develop] at an undetermined time in the future. Because the severity of many diseases—such as sickle cell anemia and spina bifida—varies widely among individuals, a genetic prediction cannot foretell how disabling the disease will be for a specific person."

> " While 42 states provide some level of protection against genetic discrimination in health insurance, and 21 states have similar statutes [laws] for employment, most of these laws are incomplete. . . . In all cases, state and federal laws have primarily addressed the unlawful use of genetic data, sidestepping the question of whether employers and insurance companies should have access to genetic information in the first place. "

—COUNCIL FOR RESPONSIBLE GENETICS, 2007

News

SECTION A

May 21, 2008

Your genes, your privacy

From the Pages of USA TODAY More than 1,100 tests look for genetic links to various diseases.

During the years it has taken Congress to come up to speed on the issue and work out compromises with the business community, many states have passed laws that bar genetic discrimination by employers or health insurers.... [The Genetic Information Nondiscrimination Act] ... is the first to set a national standard. It's not perfect. Backers focused on employment and health insurance, but at least for now did not cover disability or life insurance. And the bill's provisions won't take effect for as long as 18 months, while federal officials write the necessary regulations.

But it's a crucial step forward. Sen. Edward Kennedy, D-Mass., one of the chief sponsors, calls it the first civil rights legislation of the new century, and he's right. Congress often acts long after civil rights abuses have become intolerable and widespread; in this case, lawmakers are ahead of the curve.

—Opinion Page

NEW LEGISLATION

On May 21, 2008, President George W. Bush signed into law the Genetic Information Non-discrimination Act (GINA). The bill was intended to protect all people in the United States from genetic discrimination. Insurance companies, for example, may not give reduced coverage to people who have tested positive for a predisposition to certain diseases. Employers and insurance companies cannot require a person to get genetic testing. Employers may not discriminate against future or current employees based on the results of their genetic tests. The law did not take effect immediately, however. Some parts of the law dealing with health insurance took effect in May 2009. Parts of the law dealing with employers took effect in November 2009.

However, some people still think that the law does not go far enough. GINA covers health insurance. But it does not cover possible genetic discrimination for life insurance. It does not include protection for people seeking disability insurance or long-term care insurance. GINA also applies only to employers who have more than fifteen employees. And the law does not cover members of the U.S. military.

GENES FOR GOOD SPORTS?

Competition runs high in sports such as bicycle racing, professional boxing, and the Olympic Games. Participants train for years to build up their muscles, their speed, and their stamina. They eat healthy foods and get the proper rest to perform well in these demanding sports. But some athletes want to have an unfair advantage over other participants. Some athletes have taken performance-enhancing drugs such as testosterone and anabolic steroids. They take these drugs to

Above: Two athletes train outside of Flagstaff, Arizona, for the Olympics. Athletes spend years becoming the best they can be, but some take shortcuts in the form of steroids and other drugs. Some people fear that in the future athletes will use genetic technologies as shortcuts too.

Above: A chemist loads athletes' urine samples into a spectrometer to test for illegal drug use. This lab in Los Angeles is one of two facilities in the United States approved by WADA to test athletes for banned substances.

pump up their muscles. But the drugs cause side effects that can include high cholesterol, hair loss, acne, and possible violent behavior. Because these drugs give athletes an unfair advantage, they are illegal in competitive sports. Blood tests and urine tests are routinely performed on athletes before competitions to screen for these illegal drugs.

Organizations such as the World Anti-Doping Agency (WADA) and the United States Anti-Doping Agency (USADA) monitor any developments in drugs that athletes might use to cheat at sports.

Will athletes use the products of the new genetic technologies to add to their future performances? Will there be tests to monitor the use of these products? Some people think this could happen soon. In March 2002, WADA sponsored a meeting at the Banbury Center at the Cold Spring Harbor Laboratory on Long Island, New York. Scientists from the laboratory met with authorities on the use of performance-enhancing substances in sports. They discussed whether the possibility of gene enhancement in sports could become a reality in the near future. Scientists at the meeting concluded that the use of genes to enhance athletic performance is not something that will happen any time soon. Other meetings were held in Sweden in 2005 and in Russia in 2008. Dr. Olivier Rabin, WADA's science director, said, "Most experts do not think that gene transfer is being used by athletes yet. But . . . some athletes may be tempted to use it one day to enhance their performance. That is why WADA takes the issue so seriously."

GENES FOR VICTORY?

In 1998, just two days before the start of the 1998 Tour de France bicycle race, customs officials at the border crossing between France and Belgium stopped a man with one of the cycling teams preparing to compete. When they searched his car, they discovered erythropoietin (EPO) as well as other banned substances.

During strenuous sports, such as bicycling, an athlete's muscles need oxygen. Athletes who want to cheat by having oxygen-rich blood coursing through their veins sometimes have an injection of EPO. The kidneys produce this hormone when there are low levels of oxygen in body tissues. EPO causes bone marrow to produce increased levels of red blood cells. With more red blood cells, the body can absorb more oxygen.

TESTING FOR ENGINEERED HORMONE ABUSE

The use of injected EPO gives an athlete an unfair advantage. However, EPO can also cause serious physical problems or even death. When the hormone stimulates the body to produce extra red blood cells, the blood becomes thicker. The heart has to pump much harder to circulate the blood. If the blood is too thick, it will not be able to circulate through the blood vessels. If this happens, an athlete could suffer a stroke or a heart attack. Or a person could die.

A member of WADA, Dr. Gary I. Wadler observed a suspicious connection between the deaths of some strong, healthy athletes a few years after the introduction of EPO as a therapy for anemia sufferers. Possibly eighteen Belgian and Dutch cyclists who died suddenly of heart attacks in the late 1980s may have used EPO.

Some athletes have sacrificed their futures by using illegal performance enhancers. During the 2008 Beijing Olympics, more than five thousand tests for illegal enhancement drugs were conducted on Olympic athletes. The rules state that if there is evidence of prohibited enhancement, athletes would be disqualified from the Olympic Games. After testing, six athletes were disqualified.

CHAPTER SIX

The Cloning Controversy

Another genetic controversy has arisen over the ethical issues of cloning animals and possibly cloning of humans. Clones are identical copies of an organism. Clones have exactly the same DNA in exactly the same order on the chromosome. Identical twins are an example of natural human clones. When a man's sperm cell fertilizes a woman's egg cell, it causes the egg cell to divide. Usually, this dividing egg cell grows and becomes one embryo. After nine months, one human child is born. However, occasionally a fertilized egg splits into two separate but identical halves. Each half then develops into a separate child. But since the two separate embryos originally started out as the same sperm cell and egg cells, the resulting children will look alike and have the same genetic material. (Sometimes two separate eggs are fertilized by two different sperm cells. Although the two eggs develop at the same time, the two resulting children will have different DNA. They are called fraternal twins.)

Actresses Mary-Kate *(left)* and Ashley Olsen are identical twins, meaning they have identical DNA. Identical twins are natural human clones.

Natural clones also occur in the animal world. In the early 1900s, a German scientist named Hans Spemann took a strand of hair and used it as a small noose to tease apart the cells of a two-celled salamander embryo. Each of the cells grew. Spemann had caused one embryo to turn into two normal salamanders. In 1938 he proposed removing a nucleus from one cell and then putting a nucleus from another cell into the empty cell. This is the basis of modern cloning techniques. However, the technology was not advanced enough to permit him to successfully complete this cloning experiment.

In 1952 two U.S. scientists, Robert Briggs and Thomas King, succeeded in cloning frogs by transplanting DNA from tadpole embryos. Then, in 1962, John Gurdon took the nucleus from the intestinal cells of adult South African frogs and cloned them.

THE BIG BREAKTHROUGH

The biggest breakthrough in the science of cloning came on July 5, 1996, with the birth of a lamb named Dolly. Her birth wasn't announced until February 1997 in the journal *Nature*. Although animals had been cloned before, Dolly made headlines. She was cloned from a mammary cell— a cell that produces milk—of an adult female sheep. Before Dolly's birth, many scientists had theorized that it was impossible to clone a mammal with adult cells. When an egg cell is fertilized by a sperm cell, an embryo starts to grow. For a short time, the cells that form can grow into

Above: Dolly at seven months old. The birth of Dolly—a cloned sheep—made headlines around the world in 1997.

any kind of cell, such as heart or liver cells. But as the embryo continues growing, these cells eventually "choose" to grow into only one type of cell. For a long time, scientists thought that it would be impossible to clone an animal using cells that had already "turned off" the ability to grow into any type of cell. But Dolly proved them wrong.

NUCLEAR TRANSFER

Dolly was cloned by a process called nuclear transfer. Scientist Ian Wilmut and colleagues at the Roslin Institute, near Edinburgh, Scotland, took mammary cells from the udder of a type of white sheep, called a Finn Dorset ewe. The scientists placed the cells in a laboratory dish called a petri dish. They starved the cells so they wouldn't divide. Next, they took an egg from another breed of sheep, called a Scottish Blackface. The nucleus (which contains DNA) was then removed from the Scottish Blackface sheep's egg. Finn Dorset sheep and Scottish Blackface sheep have very different coloration. This would make it obvious

whether the resulting lamb was the genetic daughter of the all-white sheep or the one with a black face.

Wilmut and his team put the enucleated (emptied of its nucleus) egg into a petri dish together with a mammary cell. They caused the cells to join by giving them a small pulse of electricity. Another small amount of electricity caused the joined cells to grow into an embryo. Wilmut and his colleagues allowed the embryo to grow for about one week. Then it was implanted into a third sheep, also a Scottish Blackface, to grow inside its womb. This ewe, a surrogate mother, later gave birth to Dolly. And Dolly was born a Finn Dorset sheep, identical to the ewe whose mammary cells had provided the DNA for the experiment.

When Wilmut and his colleagues cloned Dolly, she wasn't the result of just one egg, one nucleus, and one surrogate mother. Out of 277 ewes' egg cells that received transplanted DNA, only 29 embryos survived for six days or more. Out of these, only 13 resulted in pregnancies. Dolly was the only lamb to result in a live birth.

Spurred on by the cloning of Dolly, researchers at the University of Hawaii succeeded in cloning mice in 1997. Teruhiko Wakayama, a Japanese student at the university, took cumulus cells from female mice. These cells surround the eggs in ovaries. (Ovaries are the female reproductive organs that release one egg about every month.) Wakayama injected the nucleus from a cumulus cell directly into a mouse egg that had had its nucleus removed. Wakayama succeeded in cloning a mouse. Then he made clones of the clone for a total of fifty mice. He and his team announced the results in 1998.

CLONING CATS AND DOGS

On December 22, 2001, a calico kitten was delivered by cesarean section (cutting through the mother's abdomen and womb to remove the baby). Scientists at Texas A&M University had cloned the kitten. They named it CC (for carbon copy). The scientists had taken DNA from an adult female cat named Rainbow. Then they removed the DNA from another cat's egg cell. They then replaced it with Rainbow's DNA. When the egg cell started dividing and became an embryo, they implanted it into the uterus of Allie, the surrogate mother cat. The embryo grew inside Allie until it was ready to be born. CC is a calico, but she does not look exactly like her genetic mother, Rainbow. The distinctive pattern on a calico's fur is determined in part by genetics. But it is also affected by other factors, such as the environment and how the cat fetus grows in its mother's womb.

Before their success with CC, the researchers had first completed 188 nuclear transfer procedures. The researchers had transferred the DNA from the skin cells of adult cats into eggs with their nuclei removed. Only eighty-two embryos resulted from those 188 nuclear transfers. These embryos were implanted into seven female cats. Only one out of the eighty-two implanted embryos resulted in a pregnancy. But there were problems, and the pregnant cat miscarried. Only then did the researchers use DNA from feline ovary cells. Of the five embryos they obtained by using egg cells, one cat, CC, was born.

In 2005 South Korean scientist Hwang Woo-Suk and his colleagues succeeded in creating the first cloned dog, an Afghan hound named Snuppy. Created with the DNA of a male Afghan hound, Snuppy was conceived by a yellow Labrador surrogate mother. The scientists used nearly two thousand eggs to create one thousand embryos. Of all these embryos, just one resulted in Snuppy's live birth.

In May 2008, scientists used Snuppy's sperm to artificially inseminate (make pregnant) two female dogs, also clones. Ten puppies were born, and nine survived. Lee Byung-Chun led a team of South Korean researchers in this experiment. He said that this was the first successful breeding of cloned dogs as parents.

Many people who love their pets grieve when their cat or dog grows old and dies. Cloning may be a way to obtain another animal that looks like their dead pet. In August 2008, five pit bull puppies were born. They are clones of the deceased pet of a U.S. woman. She paid a Korean company, RNL Bio, to make copies of her beloved dog Booger, who she said once saved her life. But some people see this as unnecessary and unethical. The Humane Society of the United States (HSUS) "condemns the commercial cloning of companion animals." They cite an existing problem with overpopulation of dogs and cats. Many of these animals are destroyed when homes cannot be found for them. HSUS states that cloning is not a perfect science and carries dangers for the animals involved. The society adds, "Cloning can only replicate the pet's genetics, which influence but do not determine . . . physical attributes or personality. In fact, a pet's personality . . . is the trait least likely to be replicated by cloning. In addition, there is no guarantee the cloned companion animal will even physically resemble the original pet."

USA TODAY Snapshots®

A look at statistics that shape the nation

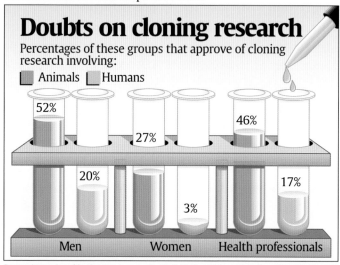

Doubts on cloning research

Percentages of these groups that approve of cloning research involving:

■ Animals ▪ Humans

52%

27%

46%

20%

17%

3%

Men   Women   Health professionals

Source: Aragon Consulting Group   By Cindy Hall and Marcy E. Mullins, USA TODAY, 1998

HUMAN CLONING?

In 2004 Hwang Woo-Suk and colleagues announced a breakthrough in cloning science. Hwang said he and his team had cloned the first human embryo. They intended to use cloned human embryos to obtain new stem cells. The following year, he reported that he had cloned more than thirty human embryos and eleven stem cell lines (stem cells that can grow continuously, under laboratory conditions, outside a living organism).

These announcements raised hopes that stem cell cures for various diseases might soon be a reality. But eventually, some people became suspicious of Hwang's claims. In December 2005, an investigative panel at South Korea's Seoul National University reported preliminary findings. They said that Hwang's scientific team had made up data in his papers. Hwang resigned his post at the university. In January 2006, the university panel's final report said both of Hwang's papers on stem cells had falsified information.

But his claim of cloning a dog, Snuppy, was in fact true.

SHOULD SCIENTISTS CLONE HUMANS?

If human cloning becomes possible, infertile couples might be able to realize their dream of having children. Human cloning might also save the life of an existing child who is dying because of a failing organ. If a clone of the child could be born soon enough, doctors could transplant an organ to the sick child.

But many questions arise about human cloning. Although a clone made with the nuclear transfer method starts with an egg that has had its own nuclear DNA removed, another kind of DNA may still remain. Inside the cytoplasm of cells are small, rod-shaped structures called mitochondria. These structures provide usable energy for the cell. Mitochondria have their own individual DNA, which is different from that in a cell's nucleus. This mitochondrial DNA gets passed from a mother to her children. What would happen if the egg used in cloning had defective mitochondrial DNA?

If a surrogate mother is used, another question about her contribution to the clone arises. The way she eats and exercises will affect the development of the embryo growing inside her. What would happen if a surrogate mother suddenly became sick? How would her health affect the embryo? What if she didn't lead a healthy lifestyle? What if she smoked, drank alcohol, or ate an unhealthy diet? These details would undoubtedly affect the clone.

PROGRAMMED TO FAIL?

Some critics of cloning point out that cloning is unpredictable. Dolly and other cloned animals were the result of many, many tries. Most of the eggs scientists tried to grow into clones did not grow into embryos. Of those that did, few resulted in actual pregnancies. Many of these pregnancies didn't result in a live birth. And cloned animals that survive are sometimes larger than usual or deformed. Since it takes so many tries to get a successful clone, some people ask, wouldn't it be unethical to experiment with human clones? Many of these embryos could die. And any children that might be born could have physical problems.

Critics also worry that clones may not live as long as people conceived in the usual way. They point out that Dolly was cloned from a cell from a six-year-old sheep. Dolly's cells had telomeres that were 20 percent shorter than sheep conceived in the natural way. (Telomeres are sections of DNA found at the ends of chromosomes. They may be involved in the aging process. As chromosomes divide, their telomeres become shorter.) At a certain point, after a cell has divided many times, very little, if anything, is left of the telomere, and the cell dies.

Opponents of cloning point out that Dolly developed arthritis at a younger age than regular sheep. Dolly also developed a serious lung disease when she was only six years old. This disease also normally occurs in older sheep. Scientists decided to have her put to sleep because the lung disease would only get worse. That makes one wonder whether human clones would develop diseases that normally occur only in older people and therefore live shorter lives.

THE LIFE OF A HUMAN CLONE

If scientists succeed in cloning humans one day, how would being a clone affect a person's outlook on life? Clones could peer at their genetic look-alikes and see how they would appear as they age. Would this upset them or make them happy? If a clone found out that her mother died of a genetic disease, this news would probably cause concern for her future health.

What about the psychological aspects of future human cloning? If a clone looks exactly like her mother, would people expect her to behave just like her mother? *Time* magazine online asked Ian Wilmut, who developed Dolly, if he would consider cloning himself one day. Wilmut said he would not. He said that people would "expect the clone to be like the original, and put expectations and limitations on

USA TODAY Snapshots®

A look at statistics that shape the nation

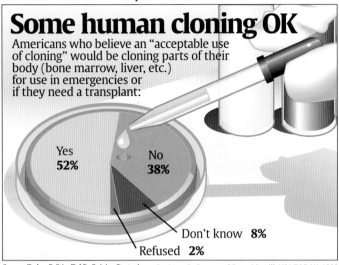

Some human cloning OK

Americans who believe an "acceptable use of cloning" would be cloning parts of their body (bone marrow, liver, etc.) for use in emergencies or if they need a transplant:

Yes
52%

No
38%

Don't know **8%**

Refused **2%**

Source: TechnoPolitics/Public Opinion Strategies   By Anne R. Carey and Dave Merrill, USA TODAY, 1998

them. . . . I think people should be wanted as individuals."

Some opponents of cloning say a clone could never be exactly the same as the person whose DNA was copied. People's environments, not just their genes, shapes who they are. A person born in a big, polluted city in a cold climate, with cruel parents would be a different person from a clone born twenty years later in a tropical climate with pure water and fresh air and kind parents. Even identical twins don't have exactly the same interests. One might enjoy classical music, while her twin prefers jazz.

STEM CELL RESEARCH

Many people are excited about the future possibilities of stem cell research. Researchers hope these cells will lead to cures for Alzheimer's disease, Parkinson's disease, diabetes, spinal cord injuries, and much more. But some aspects of this technology are controversial. Many scientists want to use human embryos to obtain stem cells for research. When the stem cells are removed, the embryos are destroyed.

But a compromise might be on the way. In 2007 Shinya Yamanaka and his team at Kyoto University in Japan, together with researchers working at the lab of James Thomson at the University of Wisconsin in Madison, succeeded in transforming human skin cells into cells that resembled stem cells. And in 2008, another scientist, Hajime Ogushi, working at Japan's National Institute of Advanced Industrial Science and Technology, said his team had created stem cells by using cells from the extracted wisdom teeth of a ten-year-old girl. These methods do not offer immediate success. But they do offer the promise of future cures without the controversy of destroying embryos for stem cells.

British researchers were the first to study embryonic stem cells (ES) in mice. In 1998 U.S. scientists began studying them. Some scientists use embryonic stem cells obtained from embryos left over from in vitro fertilization. In vitro fertilization is designed to help couples who are not fertile, or able to bear children. The technique starts with the prospective mother taking drugs that cause her ovaries to produce many eggs. The scientist, called a fertility specialist, then takes these eggs from the woman's ovaries and adds them to a solution in a petri dish. The solution keeps the eggs alive and healthy. Then the scientist adds sperm from the prospective father to the eggs. Sperm is sometimes directly injected into the eggs. Then the eggs and sperm go into an incubator (a chamber that provides a controlled environmental condition) to keep them alive. After one day or so, the sperm fertilizes the eggs.

After two or three days, the fertilized eggs grow into embryos. The scientist places several embryos inside the prospective mother's uterus—the female reproductive organ where embryos are nurtured and develop. Not every embryo will grow into a fetus, so implanting more than one increases the chances that the woman will give birth. On occasion, a woman will give birth to twins or triplets or even octuplets, as was the case of a woman in California in 2009.

If more embryos are produced than needed, the fertility specialist will often freeze and store them for possible future use. Because frozen embryos can last for years, they can be implanted later if a woman decides to have more children through this method.

Some people who go to in vitro fertilization clinics decide they do not want more children. The clinic can discard the remaining frozen embryos. Because these embryos can potentially grow into a human being, controversy exists about scientists using these discarded embryos to obtain stem cells.

OBTAINING AND STUDYING STEM CELLS

When an embryo is about five days old, it is called a blastocyst. A blastocyst contains about a hundred cells. Many of them are stem cells. At this stage, each stem cell can turn into any other cell. Scientists remove the stem cells from the blastocyst. They put them into a petri dish, where they are given nutrients so they can multiply.

Why do some scientists want to study embryonic stem cells? Scientists still don't understand how embryonic stem cells have the ability to develop into different types of cells. But they hope to learn more. They want to use these undifferentiated cells to repair or replace damaged organs or other parts of the body.

Some scientists also hope to test new drugs on stem cells. If researchers could coax these undifferentiated cells to grow into specific cells, they could see how the cells respond to certain new drugs. This work might shorten the amount of time it takes to learn whether a drug works well on certain parts of the body, without testing it on animals or people.

Studying embryonic stem cells might also allow researchers to learn more about how a human embryo develops. This in turn might help scientists prevent or treat birth defects. But perhaps the most hoped-for result of studying these cells would be for curing human diseases. If a person needed a transplant, for example, perhaps stem cells could be grown into organs that could save lives. If an organ, such as the heart or the brain, was damaged or diseased, stem cells injected into the organ might replace the cells that were lost.

ETHICS OF STEM CELL RESEARCH

Stem cell therapy holds the promise of developing cures for many devastating diseases. Yet it remains a very controversial topic. When scientists remove stem cells from blastocysts, the embryo is destroyed. For people who believe that life begins at conception, this means the destruction of a human life.

Opponents of stem cell research believe that scientists should use adult stem cells rather than embryonic stem cells. But supporters of embryonic stem cell research point out that adult stem cells are already specialized. Therefore, they can't be used to repair

> **"When human beings in the weakest and most vulnerable state of their existence are selected, abandoned, killed or utilized as mere 'biological material' how can one deny that they're being treated not as 'someone' but as 'something,' thus calling into question the very concept of the dignity of the human person?"**
>
> **—POPE BENEDICT XVI,** *DIGNITAS PERSONAE (HUMAN DIGNITY),* DECEMBER 12, 2008

> " **Many scientists say cells taken from human embryos offer the most promise of being used to develop therapies for Parkinson's, diabetes and other diseases. Some scientists have found cells taken from adults also have lifesaving potential.** "
>
> —MIMI HALL,
> USA TODAY NOVEMBER 17, 2008

every part of the human body. Critics of using embryos point out that stem cells from umbilical cord blood have already helped children with blood diseases. Dr. Joanne Kurtzberg of Duke University Medical Center in Pennsylvania and her colleagues are working on using stem cells from umbilical cord blood to repair defects in organs. Scientists in Thailand have removed stem cells from the blood of people with impaired hearts. The scientists then grew the cells inside their laboratory. When they injected these newly grown cells into the patients' hearts, their conditions seemed to improve.

Is it ethical for researchers to grow human embryos for the sole purpose of cultivating stem cells? This process is called research cloning, or therapeutic cloning. Some people view these cells as a mere mass of cells, while others see them as living beings.

Are the claims made for cures through stem cell research just hype, or do they hold real promise? Some scientists think we can't afford to stop research on these cells because it holds out hope for millions of people. Hans Keirstead, a scientist at the University of California, Irvine, looks forward to the first clinical trial of embryonic stem cell therapy in the near future. In 2005 Keirstead published a study showing that a therapy he had derived from human embryonic stem cells could make partially paralyzed rats walk. In early 2009, the FDA gave permission for the first clinical trial of the treatment in human beings with spinal cord injuries. As Claudia Kalb, a medical writer for *Newsweek* magazine, put it, "The science is about to leave the petri dish."

Still, the debate about embryonic stem cell research is not over. "I think a lot of false expectations are being raised about the potential of embryonic stem cells to cure diseases," comments Dr. Stuart Newman, professor of cell biology and anatomy at New York Medical College. "In my opinion, stem cell cures for Alzheimer's and diabetes are very unlikely. Prospects for the repair of spinal cord injuries or of the damaged heart with stem cells are more likely, but in this regard, research on adult stem cells looks even more promising at this time than that on embryonic stem cells."

But the National Institutes of Health, a U.S. government agency, disagrees. It states that embryonic stem cells offer "the possibility of ... [treating] ... diseases, conditions and disabilities including ... spinal cord injury, burns, heart disease ... [and other diseases.]"

CONTROVERSY IN CONGRESS

In 2001 President George W. Bush was confronted with an ethical dilemma. Should he allow embryonic stem cell research to continue? He discussed the matter with many scientists, bioethicists, religious leaders, and others. He heard both pro and con arguments. In the end, Bush decided to allow federal funding for embryonic stem cell research, but only on the existing sixty stem cell lines.

He thought his decision would allow stem cell research to continue without destroying more embryos. He said, "This allows us to explore the promise and potential of stem cell research without crossing a fundamental moral line, by providing taxpayer funding that would

www.usatoday.com

USA TODAY

Life

SECTION D

August 28, 2008

Researchers 'reprogram' pancreas cells in mice

From the Pages of
USA TODAY

Call it "Extreme Makeover, the Cellular Edition."

A team of biologists has turned mouse pancreas tissue into specialized cells, the same ones that go missing in juvenile diabetes.

The mouse study, led by Qiao Zhou of the Harvard Stem Cell Institute, opens a new avenue to "regenerative medicine," in which physicians remake patient cells into tissues that can be used to treat diabetes and heart and brain ailments.

"We 'flipped' the cells from one state to another," says Harvard's Douglas Melton, senior author of the study.... Zhou and his colleagues found that only three genes trigger the "reprogramming" of the cells. Melton warns, however, that treatments with these reprogrammed cells must be tested in human cells and are likely years away.

In the three-year study, researchers infected the pancreases of dozens of two-month-old mice with a virus that contained three genes active in insulin-producing beta cells. More than twenty percent of the infected pancreas cells turned into beta cells, a rate hundreds of times better than past attempts to turn embryonic stem cells into such specialized tissues.

Juvenile diabetics and some adult ... diabetes patients suffer from a lack of beta cells. If ordinary pancreas cells could be converted into beta cells, they offer a path to treatment.... Doctors would still need to prevent patient immune systems from destroying these new cells.

—Dan Vergano

sanction or encourage further destruction of human embryos that have at least the potential for life." Bush pledged $250 million in government funding that year for research on stem cells from umbilical cords, placentas, and adults.

But some scientists disagreed with Bush. Kevin Eggan, a researcher at Harvard University, said, "I believe the moral obligation we have to treat diseases and relieve suffering outweighs our obligation to the embryo." He believes that scientists have the responsibility to do research to stop human suffering.

In February 2005, Representative Mike Castle of Delaware introduced the Stem Cell Research Enhancement Act. It would require the National Institutes of Health to give more funding for stem cell research, even if the stem cells came from embryos. In July 2006, Congress passed that bill. It was intended to give millions of dollars to embryonic stem cell research. That bill would have in effect lifted Bush's 2001 ban. President Bush vetoed the bill. This prevented the bill from becoming a law.

However, Bush did sign another bill that had passed the same week by both the House of Representatives and the Senate. That bill bans the creation of human embryos to develop human organs. One

Support for stem cell research varies

About 14% of U.S. adults say federal limits on controversial embryonic stem cell research should end. But that opinion varies by region — as does support among governors in 11 states with the most biotech companies:

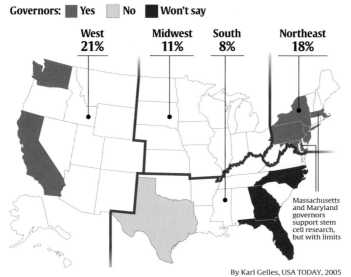

Governors: ■ Yes ▨ No ■ Won't say

| West 21% | Midwest 11% | South 8% | Northeast 18% |

Massachusetts and Maryland governors support stem cell research, but with limits

By Karl Gelles, USA TODAY, 2005

Source: USA TODAY/CNN/Gallup telephone poll of 1,015 adults in October.
Margin of error: ±7 percentage points.

longtime believer in the promise of stem cells is Nancy Reagan, the wife of the late president Ronald Reagan. He had suffered from Alzheimer's disease in the years before his death. She once said, "I just don't see how we can turn our back on [stem cell research]—there are just so many diseases that can be cured, or at least helped. We have lost so much time already."

In January 2009, President Barack Obama said he wanted legislation in Congress to permit federal funding of stem cell research and to overturn the Bush ban. He said, "I like the idea of the American people's representatives expressing their views on an issue like this." Obama seeks a bipartisan consensus in Congress that such research is ethical and potentially lifesaving. He said that if stem cell research can bring hope for victims of degenerative diseases, such as Parkinson's and Alzheimer's, "I think that sends a powerful message."

On March 9, 2009, President Obama lifted Bush's strict limits on stem cell research. The new executive order seeks to advance the research and to draw a strict line against human cloning. Obama said he realized that "many thoughtful and decent people are conflicted about, or strongly oppose, this research." But "the majority of Americans have come to a consensus that we should pursue this research; that the potential it offers is great, and with proper guidelines and strict oversight the perils can be avoided." Senator Edward M. Kennedy of Massachusetts, a longtime health-care expert, said "With today's executive order, President Obama has righted an immense wrong done to the hopes of millions of patients."

CHAPTER SEVEN

Should We Patent Life?

In 1980 the U.S. Patent and Trademark Office (USPTO) granted a unique patent to a General Electric scientist named Ananda Chakrabarty. A patent is a right granted to an inventor by the USPTO. A patent names the inventor as the sole owner of a product or process. No one else is allowed to produce or use the invention without the permission of the inventor for a period of up to twenty years.

The USPTO judges whether or not to grant patents by asking: First, is the invention useful in a practical way? Second, is it novel—new and not known or used before? Third, is it non-obvious—not something that could be made easily by someone who is familiar with this type of invention? Lastly, the person or company seeking the patent must describe the invention in detail so people can use the invention for its intended purpose.

What made the Chakrabarty patent so remarkable was that his invention was a life-form. He had genetically engineered a new type of bacteria. Chakrabarty knew that oil spills can be disastrous. He set out to combine the qualities of a number of different

Left: Ananda Chakrabarty stands in front of the Supreme Court of the United States with his patent, the Supreme Court decision in his favor, and his newly patented bacteria.

bacteria. All had the ability to devour crude oil. The strains he worked with were all from the same family, Pseudomonas. By genetically manipulating four different strains, Chakrabarty created what he hoped would be a super oil eater to clean up oil spills quickly and efficiently.

When Chakrabarty applied for a patent in 1971, the U.S. patent office refused on the grounds that living things cannot be patented. Chakrabarty appealed the decision. After years of debate, the case went to the Supreme Court. In 1980, in a 5–4 vote, the Court ruled that Chakrabarty should receive his patent because the new microbe he developed from bacteria had not existed in nature before. The microbe was therefore the scientist's invention. But the product was never marketed because it didn't work as intended outside the laboratory. Nevertheless, the granting of this patent caused great controversy about whether life-forms should be patented.

In the twenty-first century, some people believe life-forms that are redesigned through genetic engineering are inventions. These people believe the creators of these inventions deserve protection from competitors who could copy them. Others contend that life is too sacred to be viewed in the same way as machinery or manufacturing. Chakrabarty's microbe proved to be just the first of several life-forms to be patented.

ETHICAL ISSUES

In 1988 the OncoMouse, the first genetically modified mammal, was patented in the United States. Two separate patents cover Harvard's OncoMouse. One expired in February 2009, but the other will last until July 2016. In Europe and Canada, scientists also attempted to patent transgenic mice, but the European Union and Canadian courts strongly opposed this type of patenting. In 2002 the Supreme Court of Canada rejected the proposed OncoMouse patent. In 2004 the European Union, after much debate, allowed a patent for the OncoMouse.

Other patents for transgenic animals followed. As higher

forms of life become patented, new ethical issues arise. Dr. Stuart Newman of New York Medical College and Nachama Wilker, former executive director of the Council for Responsible Genetics in Massachusetts, say that "the idea that transgenic animals are inventions has been supported in large part by a widely held, but incorrect concept of the part that genetic material, DNA, plays in defining the traits of living organisms. If the point of view is accepted that DNA is the 'blueprint' or the 'program' that defines all of an organism's traits, then it stands to reason that making a precisely described modification in an organism's DNA will lead to a well-defined set of changes in the organism's set of traits. However, nothing can be further from the truth."

Newman and Wilker say scientists cannot accurately predict which traits will be produced when an organism is altered. As an example, they cite the case of the human growth hormone gene that caused different reactions in different animals. Newman and Wilker conclude that "the idea that a transgenic animal is an invention . . . [or] . . . a product of human ingenuity with definable and reproducible novel qualities is based on an extreme oversimplification of the relation of gene to traits."

The Biotechnology Industry Organization (BIO) in Washington, D.C., disagrees. In a pamphlet titled *Animals, People, and Biotechnology*, BIO states, "Patenting animals is not ethically different . . . from owning them. Owning animals is legitimate and traditional in our culture. Of course, patented animals should be treated with care and compassion, as should all animals."

Another issue that Newman and Wilker raise is the tendency of biotech researchers to create more and more uniform varieties of animals. Patents are very specific about what they cover, so uniformity makes patent claims easier to enforce. Newman and Wilker caution that "this will . . . undercut the resilience of populations of farm animals when confronted with disease and climate change." So the more varieties of farm animals there are, the more they stand a chance of having the ability to protect themselves against diseases and shifts in the environment, such as temperature changes. Each variety has different strengths and weaknesses. Each reacts to distress in its own unique way. A disease that may destroy one variety may have little effect on another.

PATENTS ON CELL LINES?

In the 1990s, the National Institutes of Health attempted to patent a wide range of cell lines found in various indigenous peoples throughout the world. Researchers found that these people often carried viruses or genes that would help scientists. For example, a cell line was taken from a young man from the Solomon Islands. People from that region are known to carry viruses related to a form of leukemia. The NIH attempted to patent the cell line. However, government pressure caused them to remove their application. These attempts to patent the genetic structure of indigenous people caused a heated debate over an individual's right to their own bodies and genetic materials.

In November 2008, the Havasupai Nation in Arizona filed a lawsuit against Arizona State University for illegal use of their blood samples. Members of the Havasupai had willingly given blood samples to the university for diabetes research. But the university had tested the blood for more than diabetes. It had tested for schizophrenia, migration patterns, and potential inbreeding. The university even sent the blood samples to other researchers around the United States.

The Havasupai considered this a violation of their rights. They had not given the university permission to conduct additional tests or to send the blood samples to others. Because of this, the Havasupai feared that they would face genetic discrimination. Arizona State University, on the other hand, believed that they had a right to the blood samples. The university thought that they were simply trying to conduct scientific research on the tribe's genetic makeup.

Scientists should, in its view, be able to conduct all necessary research on their materials.

European law prevents this kind of activity. According to a European Union patent law, any invention "based on biological material of human origin" can only be patented with the "free and informed consent" of the person in which the biological material originated. This means that scientists cannot take someone's genes and consider it an invention unless the person gives them permission.

The Arizona State researchers treated the blood samples as their own invention. They did what they wanted without the consent of the Havasupai. This would be illegal in Europe. Many Native American activists in the United States would like to see a similar law enacted in the United States. Such a law would protect them from scientists who wish to harvest Native American genes and patent them as their own discoveries.

A related legal question arose in 2009 as a result of gene and testing patents. In the 1990s, Myriad Genetics obtained a patent on two genes, BRCA1 and BRCA2, possibly related to an increased risk for breast cancer and ovarian cancer. The company also obtained a patent on the test that measures that risk. The patents meant that no other companies or research laboratories could do research on these genes and doctors did not have an alternative way to test the risk factor of their patients.

In 2009, however, Genae Girard filed a lawsuit against Myriad Genetics. Girard had received a diagnosis of breast cancer in 2006. She took a genetic test to see if her genes put her at an increased risk for ovarian cancer also. When the test came back positive, she requested a second test. That's when she learned that a second opinion was impossible because of Myriad's patent ownership. Other cancer patients, organizations of pathologists, and genetic researchers joined in her lawsuit. The lawsuit involves patent law, medical science, breast cancer activism, and an unusual civil liberties argument.

Christopher A. Hansen, senior national staff counsel for the American Civil Liberties Union (ACLU), believes the problem lies with the patent office, not with Myriad. He sees the restrictions imposed by the patent as a free speech, or First Amendment issue, as well as that of patent law.

Harry Ostrer, director of the human genetics program at the New York University School of Medicine (and a plaintiff in the case), argues that many companies could perform the test faster and for less than the three thousand dollars that Myriad charges. He believes such patents limit the opportunities for other research laboratories to focus on the mysteries of still-unsolved gene variations. The plaintiffs agree that gene patents restrict the practice of medicine and new research.

However, two panels of government experts have not found that the gene and testing patents have significantly impeded either research or medical care. Approximately 20 percent of the human genome is included in various patent claims. This amounts to thousands of individual genes according to a report from the National Institutes of Health. The report warns that in the future, individual developers may find it more difficult to obtain all the necessary licenses to proceed with the next generations of tests. Meanwhile, many women who want to be tested for ovarian cancer risk simply cannot afford the Myriad test, the only one available. At this time, a court decision is pending.

PATENTING PROS AND CONS

Some people view gene patenting as necessary. They think a government-granted right helps them continue research that might improve the quality of life or even save the lives of many people. Inventors must be protected, they argue, or else competitors might steal their ideas. Some researchers worry that if they don't patent their products, then anyone can manufacture them. If that happens, the original inventor will not make a profit. If inventors won't make a profit, then they will not invest in more research.

When something is patented, its secrets must be revealed. This is why polymerase chain reaction (PCR), a patented process used in DNA testing, is known and used by many scientists. PCR is used with the permission of Hoffmann-La Roche, the pharmaceutical company holding the patent to the process. Since a patent is valid for only twenty years, once it runs out, anyone can use the technology without asking Hoffmann-La Roche for permission. While the company holds the patent, Hoffmann-La Roche can ask those using PCR to pay for the right to use its invention.

One controversial aspect of patenting life-forms is the question of broad patents. For instance, the OncoMouse patent covers every animal that has the oncogene put into it. So if scientists other than the patent holder want to conduct research using the OncoMouse or any other animal that has had the oncogene engineered into its DNA, they must ask for permission.

In most cases, the scientists will have to pay fees, called royalties, to the patents' holders. Broad patents like these differ from patents for inventions that are not alive. If someone receives a patent on a type of computer, for instance, the patent does not extend to all computers that may be invented later.

Another issue arising from patenting living organisms is the question of who owns the offspring of these plants or animals. Most inventions do not reproduce, but living things do. If a genetically altered farm animal gave birth, would farmers have to pay royalties to the patent holder? Should seeds from modified plants belong to the buyer or the seller who developed them?

An enormous controversy has arisen about patenting genetically altered seeds for food crops because it raises the possibility of farmers having to pay royalties to use them. Hope Shand argues that having a few large corporations control biological products and processes presents a threat to the world food supply and to the world's poor people. She also thinks patenting could lead to uniform plants. That could bring an end to the current variety of food crops. Uniform crops could be more vulnerable to plant diseases.

Some large agribusiness companies—large-scale farming businesses—have already received broad patents entitling them to receive payments for the use of their seeds or their patented processes. Some critics fear that such patents could lead to a standstill in research on cotton. Because of the way patent law works, even research is forbidden on a patented product without the permission of the patent holder.

Who should decide if and when patents should be issued? Are patents always for important, needed developments? When the Upjohn Company applied for a European patent on its "hairless mouse," the European Patent Office refused.

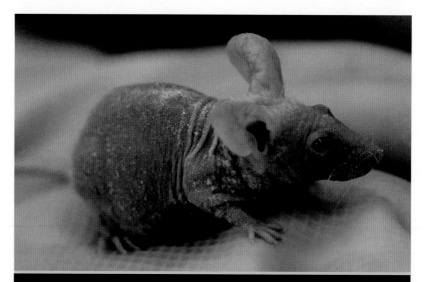

Above: Hairless mice, like this one, have been created to use in experiments. The ability to patent animals whose genes have been altered is still being debated.

The animal was genetically altered to function as a tool in finding a cure for baldness in humans. The European Patent Office decided that since the OncoMouse may be a valid research tool in the study of cancer—a life-threatening disease—it had great value to alleviate human suffering. But the office decided that the hairless mouse was not suitable for a patent, because baldness does not present a significant public health problem.

BIOPIRACY OR PROTECTING INVESTMENTS?

In the 1950s and 1960s, scientists discovered a type of bacteria that can survive very hot temperatures in the hot springs of Yellowstone National Park. An enzyme from these bacteria is used in PCR. PCR is a method of creating millions of copies of small amounts of DNA. This method is often used to get larger amounts of biological evidence from small amounts at crime scenes. Hoffmann-La Roche, the pharmaceutical company that owns the patent for PCR, has made millions of dollars every year. But none of this is paid to Yellowstone.

In 1995 two scientists at the University of Mississippi Medical Center received a patent for the use of turmeric to help heal wounds. Turmeric is a plant responsible for the bright yellow color of Indian curry. However, in 2004 the United States Patent and Trademark Office revoked the patent when some people in India proved to them that an ancient text first mentioned the use of turmeric for this purpose. So the scientists at the university were not the first to discover this use.

In India, people have been practicing a type of traditional plant-based medicine called Ayurveda for thousands of years. An article in the *San Francisco Chronicle* states that India claims that as of 2006, there were five thousand U.S. patents on medicinal plants, and of these, the vast majority were Indian plants.

Critics of patenting traditional plants call this practice biopiracy. The ETC Group defines biopiracy as "[taking] . . . genetic resources and knowledge . . . from the farming communities and peoples that have developed and nurtured those resources."

Scientists at Eli Lilly and Company developed two anti-cancer drugs from a flower called the rosy periwinkle. The flower grows in Madagascar, a large island off the eastern coast of Africa. The drug has helped to save lives. And the company has made millions of dollars in profits from sales of the drug. But no one in Madagascar shared in those profits. Many people believe that since these plants are Madagascar's resource, Madagascans should have made money from the drugs. Others argue that the money rightly belongs to the pharmaceutical company. After all, the company spent its time and money investigating the rosy periwinkle and developing a synthetic form of the flower's healing properties.

Should companies receive patents on drugs based on traditional remedies? Those in favor of these patents point out that companies spend a great deal of money developing drugs. Naturally, they want to make sure they will receive money to cover their investments. And if remote places, such as rain forests, harbor natural cures for serious diseases, shouldn't drug companies develop these cures? According to the BIO, "Scientific research . . . provides amazing promise for humankind, but it takes time and money. Therefore, biotechnology companies must protect their research investments, so that they can reach the ultimate goal of a final high-quality product."

BIO represents more than eleven hundred biotechnology companies, academic institutions, and other organizations worldwide. BIO's members research and develop health-care, agricultural, industrial, and environmental biotechnology products. The cost of creating their final products is high, says BIO. "The research and development time for commercializing plants and animals is in the decades and can cost a company tens of millions of dollars."

> **"Developing innovative drugs is a risky, time-consuming and expensive process; therefore, companies seek the protection of a patent to ensure that competitors will not immediately copy a product they have researched and developed."**
>
> —BIOTECHNOLOGY INDUSTRY ORGANIZATION, 2008

Some people think a fair way to deal with these issues would be for patent holders to share profits from sales of developed drugs with the country where the natural medicine originated. In 1992 the Convention on Biological Diversity (CBD), held in Rio de Janeiro, Brazil, concluded that all nations should have a right to their own genetic resources and should share in the benefits and profits of any developments using these. However, the ETC Group concluded in 2006 that "after more than a decade of negotiations, the CBD has yet to provide meaningful regulations to stop biopiracy." In 2008, during the CBD's ninth conference, held in Bonn, Germany, the ETC Group said that the meetings still did not provide ways to stop biopiracy.

PATENTING GENES

Many human genes, as well as parts of human genes, have already been patented. By the first decade of the twenty-first century, patents have been granted for about one-quarter of all human genes. The USPTO's guidelines say that just identifying the sequence of a gene on a human chromosome does not entitle researchers to a patent on that gene sequence. According to the USPTO, DNA "products" can be patentable only if they have been altered, purified, or isolated from their natural surroundings. If a human gene is in a person's body, it cannot be patented because it occurs as part of nature. Since genes or parts of genes wouldn't naturally occur alone, isolated from a human body, the USPTO concludes that they are then novel, or new. As of 2008, scientists have filed more than three million patent applications relating to the human genome with the USPTO. Human Genome Science patented a human gene in 2000 to fight AIDS, for example.

The ethics of companies owning the rights to human genes is still controversial. Patenting encourages researchers by rewarding them for their genetic discoveries. And this could lead to more cures. But it could also be a barrier to future research because money in the form of royalties must be paid to the patent holders.

Will genetic patenting give companies an incentive to develop even more tests for inherited diseases and eventually lead to preventive care for patients? Or will it lead to monopolies (exclusive possession or control) on some gene tests? If a large company owns a patent on a human gene and develops tests for mutations of this gene, will this drive up the

> " **By reducing life to the status of 'human inventions,' the Patent Office has, in effect, challenged the age-old belief that life on Earth is God's creation. The consequences of this new government policy are enormous and far-reaching, affecting the very meaning of life in the coming centuries.** "

—**JEREMY RIFKIN,** PRESIDENT, COUNCIL ON ECONOMIC TRENDS
USA TODAY MAY 19, 1995

price of genetic testing? Will all patients be able to afford expensive tests? Commenting on the patenting of human genetic materials, Warren Kaplan, in his article "Biotech Patenting 101" in the *GeneWatch* newsletter, said: "As concerned citizens, we should be asking the policy makers to what extent the economic cost of licenses ... between the 'gene holders' and the 'gene users' will affect the health care system and the consumer." Policy makers may hold the key to making the benefits of advanced gene therapy research available to all consumers. If the cost is not contained, such advances will be available only to those who can afford them.

PATENTS ON HUMANS?

If one life-form can be patented, can all life-forms, including humans? Can human life-forms be considered property and fall under the jurisdiction of the USPTO? Although the Thirteenth Amendment to the U.S. Constitution prohibits slavery and involuntary servitude—property rights over human beings—some

people fear that genetic modification could call into question the definition of a human being.

On January 23, 2004, a law known as the Weldon Amendment went into effect. This was the first law that banned the patenting of human embryos. The amendment was part of a longer bill that extended the ban to include patents on human fetuses and on humans who have already been born.

Some debate occurred over this bill. Some people asserted that it would set back scientific research. The year before, the USPTO director endorsed the bill in a letter to some members of Congress. He stated, "The USPTO understands the Weldon Amendment to provide ... congressional backing for the long-standing USPTO policy of refusing to grant any patent containing a claim that encompasses any member of the species *Homo sapiens* [humans] at any stage of development, including a human embryo or human fetus." In 2009 President Barack Obama's administration took a firm stand against any form of human cloning.

Gene patents get tougher

From the Pages of USA TODAY

"The Nation; Industry applauds new rule requiring applicants to specify a gene's function"

WASHINGTON — The U.S. Patent and Trademark Office is about to announce new rules aimed at making it more difficult for researchers and biotech firms to obtain patents on human and non-human genes.

The new rules have been eagerly awaited by the growing, $22 billion-a-year biotechnology industry, which already has developed dozens of tests for cancer and other diseases based on gene patents.

The policies could be announced as early as next week, says Brigid Quinn, a spokeswoman for the patent office. The office is waiting for the federal Office of Management and Budget to complete a review before issuing the rules.

Industry representatives say the new rules will help them by cutting down on frivolous applications for patents, clearing the way for significant discoveries that will benefit public health.

"This should help reassure the general public that (patent) claims made are really justified," says Philip Reilly, CEO of Interleukin Genetics, a biotech firm in Waltham, Mass. "It's a positive step."

Genes, packets of cellular chemicals that produce a body's unique characteristics, are naturally occurring substances that cannot be patented themselves. But biotechnicians who identify a gene's chemical formula can replicate the gene and reproduce it in the lab. They then can seek a patent on the "cloned" gene.

Bioethicists and some scientists say patents on genes' chemical formulas should not be permitted in the first place. "Genes are our common property, like the oceans, and shouldn't be subject to (business) control," says Jeremy Rifkin, president of the Council on Economic Trends, a science watchdog group in Washington, D.C.

Patents give inventors the right to charge fees for their work for 20 years, provided the invention's function is found to be "specific, substantial and credible," according to current rules.

The rules will require patent seekers to describe a gene's formula and its specific function. That should eliminate a current practice: claiming a gene patent based on an overly broad or frivolous use.

Critics have charged that the practice, permitted under current rules, allows some researchers to earn fees on patents they don't deserve. "You won't be able to say anymore that you spent $10,000 on a protein that you're just going to use in shampoo," says John Doll, director of examiners in the patent office's biotech section.

Industry representatives say patents encourage research by allowing businesses and others to recover costs of developing new biotech products. "Without (patents), scientific research would go forward but not nearly as quickly," says Lila Feisee, a patent law specialist for the Biotechnical Industry Organization, a trade group based in Washington, D.C. "The research allows all of us to lead better, healthier lives."

But Ben Mitchell, a bioethics professor at Trinity International University in Deerfield, Ill., says the "economic argument" shouldn't override moral concerns attached to gene patents. "Our genes are our common inheritance and the donation of our creator. They are not subject to even limited monopoly."

Since the 1980s, the Patent and Trademark Office has granted patents on about 1,000 human genes or gene fragments and about 5,000 plant or animal genes. More than 40,000 applications await action.

Applications for biotechnology and organic chemistry patents have jumped the past three years as a result of an increase in applications for patents on human and non-human genes.

—Richard Willing

BLURRING GENETIC BORDERS

Although creating blended-species creatures, called chimeras, sounds like science fiction, some scientists have already produced them. In 1984 Steen Willadsen, a Danish embryologist working at Cambridge University in Britain, succeeded in mixing embryo cells from a sheep with those of a goat. The result was a creature called a geep. It had a head that resembled a goat's but the wooly chest of a sheep.

In December 2005, biologist Fred Gage of the Salk Institute in La Jolla, California, created mice with active brain cells. They were grown from human embryonic stem cells. Gage injected human cells into fourteen-day-old mouse fetuses. He injected each of the fetuses with approximately one hundred thousand human cells. Then the fetuses were put back into their mothers' wombs. Although most of the human cells died, each mouse still contained between one hundred and several hundred of these human cells. The injected human cells grew to the size and shape of usual brain cells in mice. Before this experiment,

Below: This geep is part sheep and part goat. It has both sheep wool and goat fur covering its body.

no one was sure whether human embryonic stem cells could actually function when put into an animal. This experiment proved it could be done.

However, this experiment raises serious ethical issues. Some scientists believe there is no possibility that mice with human brain cells will think like people. But what would happen if scientists could produce a creature with an all-human brain? And if a ban is put on work like this, will it hold back cures for brain diseases? Dr. Stuart Newman comments, "I think that patenting life forms is bad policy. Patents are for inventions. If we start thinking of living organisms as inventions, then we're really blurring the line between organisms and artifacts. Eventually, this could lead us to blur the line between people and artifacts."

CHAPTER EIGHT

Who Should Regulate Genetic Engineering?

Are experiments in genetic modification safe? Who should decide what "safe" means? Should researchers and businesspeople be trusted to regulate products they intend to sell? Or should a government agency be responsible for determining the safety of genetic experiments? What role, if any, should the public play? Some people think that scientists are the experts, and the decisions should be theirs. Others think that since people's lives are affected by genetic engineering, the public should play a role in setting guidelines. These questions are not easy to answer because the technology and its by-products have such great potential for medical and scientific breakthroughs—and for utter disaster.

A RECOMBINANT MENACE?

In 2000 a group of scientists in Spain successfully cloned a deadly virus found in piglets. The virus kills 80

Left: Public debate persists about the role of consumers in choosing genetically modified products. Should companies be required to identify the use of genetically modified ingredients? Should the product be labeled? Should consumers care? Who decides?

percent of those that contract it. In January of the following year, a team of Australian scientists attempted to create a contraceptive for mice. Instead, they accidentally created a deadly version of the virus known as mousepox. It killed all the mice that were injected with it. The mousepox was so potent that it even killed half the mice that had received mousepox vaccines. So the virus killed mice that were supposed to be immune to it.

Dr. Mae-Wan Ho is a Chinese geneticist who has lectured on the dangers of genetic engineering all over the world. She claims that mixing genetic material between species is a dangerous first step toward the creation of a lethal supervirus. Such a virus could, in her view, pose a great threat to public health and safety.

In the 1970s, scientists thought that the creation of an uncontrollable, highly dangerous virus was unlikely. But in the twenty-first century, with the rapid expansion of genetic engineering facilities across the world, this possibility has become a serious concern in the scientific community. Ho is afraid that the commercial success of GMOs has pushed the field in a dangerous direction. Modern-day scientists have to work faster than ever to produce better, more profitable results in this highly competitive field. Little time is left to think about safety and potential health risks.

U.S. GOVERNMENT REGULATIONS

Several different U.S. government agencies regulate genetically altered plant and animal products, depending on the recombinant product. It became evident that biotechnology was moving toward novel commercial products, such as genetically engineered human growth hormone and human insulin. The regulatory framework was published in 1986. It included statements from the Environmental Protection Agency, the U.S. Department of Agriculture, the Food and Drug Administration, and the National Institutes of Health.

www.usatoday.com

USA TODAY

Life

SECTION D

May 19, 2003

FDA reasserts oversight of genetic engineering of animals

From the Pages of USA TODAY The government is flexing its muscles with universities involved in genetic engineering, responding to a controversy . . . in which investigators feared the offspring of transgenic pigs had entered the food supply.

The Food and Drug Administration sent a letter to seventy university presidents and chancellors last week, reminding them that scientists who are genetically engineering animals that would otherwise be used for food are required to inform the FDA and document plans for the disposal of the animals when the research is done. . . .

The letter states that "the FDA is proactively informing other universities of this incident and asking for your help to raise awareness about your collective responsibilities." It is signed by Stephen Sundlof, director of the FDA's Center for Veterinary Medicine. . . .

Says Greg Jaffe of the Center for Science in the Public Interest: "Although this letter is helpful in showing that FDA wants to regulate these animals, there are still no guidances, regulations or official pronouncements." The FDA declined further comment.

—Elizabeth Weise

Does this regulatory framework protect human health and the environment? Some people think it does not. Biologist Rebecca Goldburg, senior scientist at the Environmental Defense Fund (EDF), said, "The regulatory system is flawed in part because the Reagan administration, way back in 1986, decided that they didn't want Congress involved in this area. So they decided to regulate biotechnology under existing statutes, and as a result, in some cases, we're using laws to regulate biotechnology that just aren't appropriate for the job."

She stated that some statutes are adequate, such as the current pesticide laws. These laws are also used to regulate genetically engineered pesticides, but other statutes fall short. "Genetically engineered microorganisms are being regulated under a law for toxic chemicals. They're doing that by defining genetically engineered DNA as a new chemical." Because the law doesn't really apply, problems could arise. The statute is being used to regulate things it wasn't written to cover.

STARLINK CORN

One of the most popular foods in the world is corn. Consumers enjoy corn on the cob, popcorn, corn taco shells, and corn syrup, a common sweetener in many foods. On September 18, 2000, the *Washington Post* reported that tests ordered by biotechnology opponents found traces of StarLink corn in Kraft's taco shells sold in Washington, D.C. Four days later, in response, after confirming that the discovery was correct, Kraft removed all the taco shells

from stores. In November 2000, the FDA recalled more than three hundred corn products containing StarLink.

The biotech company Aventis Crop Science, Research Triangle Park, North Carolina, owned the patent to StarLink. The genetically altered types of corn had received approval by the EPA for use as animal feed. But they were not approved as food for humans. StarLink corn had been modified to contain a protein taken from naturally occurring bacteria, Bt. When insect pests digest the protein, they eventually die of the toxin (poison) produced in their guts. The EPA oversees, among other things, the use of pesticides in the United States. Since StarLink corn was modified to contain a biopesticide, it fell under the EPA's regulations.

Although the EPA had approved StarLink corn in 1998 as food for animals, it did not allow it as human food. The EPA was aware that the Bt protein that StarLink produces is not easily digested by humans and can survive cooking. It was also possible that the Bt protein might cause allergic reactions in people. In response to the spread of StarLink corn to foods for humans, Aventis spent millions of dollars recalling the contaminated products. The company also agreed to buy back from farmers all the corn from the year 2000 crop.

imported corn from the United States, also found traces of StarLink in its imported taco shells and recalled corn products as a result.

Because of the controversy over the genetically altered corn, Aventis decided to withdraw its registration for StarLink in

> " **Neither the USDA nor FDA inspects or monitors biotech products after the heavily regulated development and testing phase. The EPA relies on the private companies that develop a biotech product to enforce planting restrictions with farmers, instead of directly monitoring farmers itself.** "
>
> **—ELIZABETH WEISE,**
> **USA TODAY** APRIL 28, 2003

The situation escalated to an international level when the Consumers Union of Japan found traces of StarLink in snack foods for humans and also in animal feed. Japan does not allow the importation of StarLink corn. Korea, a large market for

October 2000. The corn would not be grown anymore. The EPA then said that it would not approve any genetically engineered crops for animal feed unless the crops were also found to be suitable for human consumption.

SHOULD GENETICALLY ENGINEERED FOODS HAVE LABELS?

The U.S. Food and Drug Administration does not require any genetically modified foods or foods containing GM ingredients to be labeled. However, an MSNBC poll taken in 2000 showed that 81 percent of Americans believe the government should require labeling of genetically engineered food products. In addition, the poll's results showed that 89 percent of Americans wanted the government to require safety testing of genetically modified foods before allowing them on the market. Such testing is required of any food additives. In November 2001, a study carried out by the Rutgers University Food Policy Institute showed similar results. The European Union and several other countries already require such labeling.

Above: Many companies that make organic products use labels that say their products do not contain genetically modified ingredients. Pressure is mounting to force companies that do use GM ingredients to label their products.

> **The U.S. government has called requirements to label GE foods an unfair trade restriction because it sees no functional difference between GE and non-GE foods.**
>
> —ELIZABETH WEISE,
> *USA TODAY* OCTOBER 10, 2002

The American Society of Plant Biologists (ASPB), the American Frozen Food Institute (AFFI), and agribusiness as a whole oppose mandatory labeling. These groups mount powerful campaigns against any legislation that requires labeling GE products. Daniel Bush of the University of Illinois at Urbana and president of ASPB argues that "as plant scientists, we know that many of the technologies considered unnatural ... are superior to traditional methods currently in use." He goes on to say that "mandatory labeling of targeted production methods has never before been required and we believe [it] would obscure rather than clarify important issues of food safety." The ASPB does not believe that mandatory labeling would provide "a scientifically sound and uniform standard that fully informs consumers of risks or even nutritional value."

In 2002 the state of Oregon put the question of mandatory food labeling on the ballot. The biotech industry spent $5.2 million in an effort to defeat the proposal, and it succeeded. Measure 27, as it was called, was defeated by 73 to 27 percent. But some state governments do have labeling requirements. For example, in 2005 Alaska passed a bill requiring all genetically engineered fish and fish products to be labeled.

WEAKNESSES IN REGULATION

Dr. Jane Rissler of the Union of Concerned Scientists expresses concern about the regulatory system in the United States, especially in her field—agricultural genetic engineering. "It's not adequate in two respects," she says. "It's not going to ensure the environmental safety of products, and it's not adequate to ensure food safety." Rissler's words proved true in 2006 when Bayer Liberty Link 601 (BLL 601), a USDA-approved genetically engineered rice, accidentally contaminated almost 80 percent of all conventionally grown rice in the United States.

Rissler also thinks that USDA regulations are often used inappropriately. For example, the USDA oversees novel plants that are field tested—allowed to grow in large areas outside the laboratory. "Companies petition [the] USDA to ask that they not be regulated under the Federal Plant Pesticide Act. That's what was done with the Flavr Savr tomato. But there is no threat that this is a plant pest, and it ought not to be regulated as one. It's so silly. No one ever thought there were plant pests. That's part of the weakness.

The law does not really apply." Rissler is saying that the Flavr Savr tomato was never thought of as a plant that would threaten other plants. Since there were no laws specifically created for genetically engineered plants, the tomato was regulated by a law that was made for something totally different, such as weeds that would grow fast and replace good crops.

She adds that another problem with the USDA is that it "both promotes and regulates this [bio] technology, and that's a contradictory role. The department is not paying as close attention to environmental risks as we think it should." Rissler thinks the USDA needs to involve ecologists who thoroughly understand ecological risks and have them help the agency with risk assessment. She points out that "you have a different sort of uncertainty with genetically engineered crops [than with traditionally crossbreeding crops]....With traditional breeding, you may be moving segments of chromosomes, large pieces of DNA, but it's essentially within the same genome makeup, the same chromosomal makeup. What might happen with the genetic engineering is that these genes are inserted randomly, haphazardly. Contrary to what the industry says, it's not a precise thing." Rissler emphasized that the burden of proving the safety of GE foods doesn't rest with the industry itself. She said, "The government and the industry have been too eager to assume that ... these crops are substantially equivalent to existing ones. ... But I don't think they have done the kind of testing that a lot of us would want."

DISSENT

Elizabeth Milewski of the EPA disagreed with Rissler. Milewski thinks the present regulation is adequate. She says that the expertise for evaluating different biotech products lies with each of the different agencies, whether or not those products are created through recombinant DNA technology. "The expertise for evaluating ... pharmaceuticals is at FDA, the expertise for pesticides is at EPA, and the expertise in agriculture is at USDA."

Dr. Sheldon Krimsky, professor of Urban and Environmental Policy and Planning at Tufts University, thinks there are problems with many of the current regulations. In regard to basic food issues, he thinks the FDA has the correct approach to regulating food additives because the manufacturer must prove those additives are safe before the FDA gives its approval.

In the case of genetically altered foods, however, he said the FDA has not addressed some issues. Consumers should know whether they could be affected by biofoods. But they "should also have the right to decide if they want to try them at all." Krimsky believes that labeling should be required for biofoods. "Consumers don't want to be the guinea pigs," he said, "so labeling is a key issue."

In the area of plants, which fall under the USDA, Krimsky thinks there is "less rigorous risk assessment than one might hope for." He cites a study he and a colleague conducted that investigated how plants were regulated. "We found out that a lot of the decisions that were made about risks were . . . merely . . . shrug-of-the-shoulder decisions. . . . In other words, they don't require a panorama of tests. . . . They . . . simply . . . look at the existing literature or . . . get an indication that people who have worked with these things feel they're pretty safe." He concluded, "We should go very, very slowly, in my view, and the regulations often don't require that. They respond more to commercial interests than they do to public concerns." So, according to Krimsky, regulations address the needs of biotech producers more than those of the consumers who will eventually buy these products.

Dr. Michael Fernandez, executive director of the Pew Initiative on Food and Biotechnology in Washington, D.C., commented, "Part of the strength of [the U.S. regulatory system] is the fact that it relies on existing authorities. Using these existing statutory authorities has benefits in the sense that we're familiar with them. . . . And also, the product developers who want to bring a new product to market [may] have dealt [with the agencies before.]"

Fernandez also sees some challenges in the present network of systems. "You have multiple agencies that potentially have authority over a given product. So, for example, the insect protective crops—the Bt crops [which have a genetic pesticide in the plants]—are regulated by all three agencies. The field trials are regulated both by EPA and USDA. They also have to be able to be safe for food, so FDA has to look at them as well. So this requires more coordination among the agencies. There's a potential for a disconnect."

He said that other challenges arise when some products don't fit well within any one of the existing agency's categories. For example, some plants have been genetically modified to produce pharmaceuticals. "It's a food product, but it's not intended to be in the food supply. But because it's a food crop, it's considered a food. But is it a food? Is it a drug?"

Rebecca Goldburg would like to see the U.S. regulations change in the future. "Clearly, one of the things we still need is a more stringent program for genetically engineered foods. There should be a requirement for some sort of review, rather than the provision for voluntary review." So Goldburg believes that agricultural biotech companies should be required to have their products reviewed. The current guidelines say that companies may or may not volunteer to have their genetically altered products reviewed.

Beyond the GMO food-labeling controversy, however, a 2008 report by the Government Accountability Office (GAO) claims that FDA food labeling policies for all foods are outdated and poorly enforced. According to the report, the FDA has not tested the accuracy of Nutrition Fact labels since the 1990s. They also have not thoroughly investigated the products made by overseas manufacturers. In the words of Congresswoman Rosa DeLauro of Connecticut, the report indicates that the FDA is "incapable of preventing companies from providing false or misleading information to consumers." These results, in her words, are "troubling." If the FDA is to tackle the challenge of GMOs, according to DeLauro, it will first need to address its shortcomings in the non-GMO food industry.

SYNTHETIC BIOLOGY

Synthetic biology is a technology dealing with the design and construction of new biological parts, devices, and systems as well as "the redesign of existing, natural biological systems for useful purposes," according to syntheticbiology.org. One technology that synthetic biologists are working on is the ability to "build" genes. Synthetic biologists are researching the development of bacteria that could seek out and invade cancerous tumor cells and new biological sources of renewable energy. In October 2005, the U.S. Centers for Disease Control and Prevention succeeded in re-creating the 1918 Spanish flu virus that caused the deaths of millions of people. In April 2006, scientists at the University of Wisconsin–Madison created a new type of *E. coli* bacteria.

Some people, including the Council for Responsible Genetics and the ETC Group, think there should be strict regulations of this technology. They are worried that if synthetic biologists create their own regulations, there might be some problems. In a news release written by ETC Group, a coalition of thirty-eight international organizations including scientists, environmentalists, and others called for the public to be included in the "debate, regulation and oversight of the rapidly advancing field of synthetic biology." The organizations signed an open letter to encourage synthetic biologists to drop proposals they have made for self-regulation. "Tinkering with living organisms that could be released in the environment poses a grave biosafety threat to people and the planet," said Dr. Doreen Stabinsky of Greenpeace International. The open

letter concludes: "Because of the potential power and scope of this field [synthetic biology], discussions and decisions concerning these technologies must take place ... at local, national and global levels."

The question of who should regulate the new technologies is still being debated. Scientists should not be allowed to regulate their own work. And industry cannot be allowed to regulate itself. Government agencies are often behind the cutting edge of developments. And the public wants a voice in making decisions that will eventually affect them, their children, and their environment.

Where will the "genetic revolution" lead? We are already firmly in the midst of the new technology, and the future may bring even greater strides in this field. Will we see improvements in human health and the environment? Or will we be distressed by unexpected developments, such as uncontrollable epidemics or "superweeds," and wish that we had proceeded with greater caution?

Author Jack Doyle commented, "While science and technology have produced economic growth and social improvement throughout the world, they have also spawned environmental and public health disasters." If scientists take this view, they might decide to postpone experiments until they are convinced they are safe. But can we afford to proceed at a slower pace? Fred Davison, former president of the University of Georgia, warned, "The greater risk is in not using these new tools and not using them immediately to guarantee that indeed we have a future."

Dr. Ruth Hubbard concluded that scientists and laypeople alike are affected by these technologies. Consequently, everyone should be involved in the decision making. She said, "The issues are too big and affect all of us too deeply to be left up to scientists or other sorts of experts." She added that "virtually all scientific research in this country is done at least in part at the public expense. Therefore the public should be involved in the decision about how research funds are allocated."

If we hope to direct the course of the powerful genetic technologies, we should strive to learn as much as we can about these molecular tools and then let scientists and corporations know our wishes. Only then can we truly expect to avoid the risks and enjoy the progress and the promises of our genetic future.

TIMELINE

1850 Mendel works out the basics of heredity.

1865 Mendel presents his theories on the laws of heredity.

1900 Correns, de Vries, and von Tschermak independently rediscover Mendel's laws of heredity.

1944 Avery concludes that genes are made of DNA.

1951 Wilkins and Franklin begin work with X-ray diffraction photography to study DNA.

1953 Watson and Crick discover the structure of the DNA molecule.

1970 Smith and Nathans discover restriction enzymes.

1973 Cohen and Boyer use recombinant DNA technology to cut and paste a toad gene into bacteria.

1980 The United States Patent and Trademark Office (USPTO) grants a patent to Chakrabarty for genetically engineered bacteria.

1981 Evans and Kaufman develop the first stem cell line from mice.

1988 The USPTO grants a patent for the first transgenic mammal, the OncoMouse.

1990 Anderson performs the first approved gene therapy experiments on DeSilva.

Human Genome Project begins.

1994 Flavr Savr tomato becomes the first transgenic food to be approved by the FDA and sold in the United States.

1995 Thomson and colleagues isolate the first stem cell line from a mammal (rhesus monkey).

1996 Dolly the sheep is born. Wilmut clones Dolly from an adult ewe's mammary cells.

1997 Wilmut announces Dolly's birth.

1997   Wakayama and a team of researchers succeed in cloning fifty mice.

1998   Thomson and colleagues isolate first human stem cell line.

1999   Jesse Gelsinger dies of complications from a gene therapy experiment.

2000   StarLink transgenic corn, approved only for animal consumption, is found in human food. Hundreds of corn products are recalled from supermarket shelves.

2001   Traditional varieties of Mexican maize (corn) are found to be polluted by genetically engineered corn.

CC, the first cloned cat, is born.

U.S. scientists succeed in cloning early-stage human embryos for stem cells.

President George W. Bush allows federal funding for sixty existing embryonic stem cell lines but gives no federal funding for new embryonic stem cell lines.

Bush pledges $250 million in government funding for research on the stem cells of umbilical cords, placentas, and adults that does not involve the destruction of embryos.

2003   Human Genome Project completes rough drafts for each human chromosome.

Pew Initiative on Food and Biotechnology poll shows most Americans oppose genetic engineering of animals.

California bans importation of GloFish.

2005   Hwang falsely claims to have cloned over thirty human embryos and eleven stem cell lines.

Hwang clones Snuppy, the first cloned dog.

2006   Congress passes a bill for more federal funding on embryonic stem cell research.

2006   Bush vetoes the bill on federal funding for embryonic stem cell research.

Bush signs a bill banning the creation of human fetuses for the sole purpose of providing human organs.

CC, the world's first cloned cat, mates with a male cat, Smokey, and gives birth to three healthy kittens.

2007   The J. Craig Venter Institute creates the first synthetic bacteria genome.

2008   The Genetic Information Nondiscrimination Act (GINA) becomes law.

The Newborn Screening Saves Lives Act becomes law.

Korean company RNL Bio clones five pit bull puppies from the DNA of an American woman's deceased pet.

The first cloned dog, Snuppy, becomes a father to ten cloned puppies, nine of which survive. The two mothers of the puppies are also clones.

The Vatican releases a report, *Dignitas Personae*, opposing human cloning, the use of embryos for stem cell research, and the "eugenic mentality" that can arise from genetic engineering.

2009   President Barack Obama signs an executive order to permit federal funding on stem cell research and overturn a ban imposed by President George W. Bush.

On February 25, the U.S. government implements a new law that bars discrimination by insurers and employers based on genetic test results.

Genae Girard legally challenges Myriad Genetics patents on two genes, BRAC1 and BRAC2, associated with an increased risk for breast cancer and ovarian cancer and on the testing that measures that risk.

A South Korean team creates "Ruppy," a transgenic beagle puppy that carries fluorescent genes from a sea anemone. The genes give her a red glow under special lighting.

GLOSSARY

adenine: one of the chemical bases that make up DNA; usually abbreviated as A

adult stem cells: stem cells found in the skin, blood, brain, and other parts of an adult human's body. These stem cells can produce specific cells such as more skin, blood, brain, and other cells.

agribusiness: industries involved with farming production, equipment, processing, and distribution

***Bacillus thuringiensis,* or Bt:** a common soil bacterium that produces a poison within the gut of insect pests

base: a subunit of the DNA molecule. The four bases in DNA are adenine (A), cytosine (C), guanine (G), and thymine (T).

base pair: two nucleotide bases that are bonded together in a DNA molecule

biopiracy: taking genetic resources from the traditional communities that developed them and making money on these resources without paying the native developers

biotechnology: the use of living things to serve the needs of humankind

blastocyst: an early-stage embryo, resembling a hollow ball. The inner cells of this hollow ball are embryonic stem cells.

cell: the smallest structural unit of a living organism that can grow and reproduce independently

cell line: cells that can grow continuously outside a living organism, under laboratory conditions

center of diversity: a place where wild relatives or traditional varieties of a modern crop occur

chimera: an organism that contains cells from different species

chromosomes: the rodlike structures in cells. Each chromosome can contain hundreds of thousands of genes. Different species have different numbers of chromosomes. Humans have forty-six chromosomes (twenty-three pairs) in their cells.

cloning: a technique for producing genetically identical copies of a living organism

cytoplasm: the inner matter found in cells, within the cell membrane

cytosine: one of the chemical bases that make up DNA; usually abbreviated as C

DNA (deoxyribonucleic acid): a molecule that stores the information that determines an organism's hereditary properties

E. coli (Escherichia coli bacteria): a strain of bacteria commonly found in the human intestinal tract. It is often used in laboratories as the "workhorse" of genetic engineering experiments.

embryonic stem cells: stem cells taken from early-stage embryos. These cells can turn into any other types of cells.

enzymes: proteins that affect chemical reactions in living organisms

geep: an animal created by Danish embryologist Steen Willadsen. The animal has genes from both a sheep and a goat. This is a type of chimera, an organism with cells from different species.

genes: the basic units of heredity. Genes are segments of DNA in a chromosome, which carry the hereditary information to code for the production of a protein or proteins.

gene sequencing: analyzing a gene to find the specific order of its nucleotide bases: A, C, T, and G

gene-splicing: the adding or deleting of genes from different organisms, through the use of restriction enzymes, to make new substances or organisms; also called genetic engineering, or recombinant DNA technology

gene therapy: using genetic engineering to repair damaged genes or to add corrective genes in an effort to cure a hereditary disease

genetic engineering: the adding or deleting of genes from different organisms through the use of restriction enzymes; also called gene-splicing, or recombinant DNA technology

genome: the total hereditary material contained within an organism

germ cells: reproductive cells

germ-line gene therapy: gene therapy that involves permanent changes in the hereditary characteristics of an organism

guanine: one of the chemical bases that make up DNA; usually abbreviated as G

GURTs (Genetic Use Restriction Technologies): genetic manipulation that stops plants from producing seeds that can grow into new, healthy plants. Opponents call this terminator technology, or "suicide seeds."

Huntington's disease: a hereditary disease characterized by a slow deterioration of the nervous system

ligase: an enzyme that acts like molecular "glue" in recombinant DNA technology

microbiologist: someone who studies microscopic forms of life

microinjection: the use of needles small enough to inject genetic material into individual cells

mutation: a permanent change in the inherited characteristics of an organism, caused by a change in the sequence of the As, Ts, Cs, and Gs in a DNA molecule

nucleotide base: one of the four chemical bases that compose DNA: adenine (A), cytosine (C), guanine (G), and thymine (T)

nucleus: a structure in cells that contains hereditary material

plasmids: circular pieces of DNA in bacteria

polymerase chain reaction analysis (PCR): a method of producing millions of copies of sequences of DNA. Enzymes are used to amplify, or copy over and over, small amounts of DNA.

recombinant DNA, or rDNA: the adding or deleting of genes from different organisms through restriction enzymes, to make new substances or organisms. It is also called genetic engineering, or gene-splicing.

restriction enzymes: the molecular "scissors" of genetic engineering. These enzymes can cut specific genes out of a piece of DNA.

RNA (ribonucleic acid): a molecule that is similar to DNA, but has a single strand, instead of DNA's double strands, and contains the base uracil instead of thymine, found in DNA.

selective breeding: the breeding of selected plants or animals with desired traits to produce offspring with the same characteristics

sickle cell anemia: a hereditary disease characterized by a deformity of some of the sufferer's red blood cells

somatic cell gene therapy: gene therapy that affects only the organism treated and is not passed on to its offspring

somatic cells: body cells, excluding the reproductive cells

synthetic biology: a technology that deals with redesigning existing biological systems and designing new biological parts or devices

telomere: sections of DNA at the ends of a chromosome. As chromosomes divide, telomeres become shorter.

thymine: one of the chemical nucleotide bases that make up DNA; usually abbreviated as T

tPA (tissue plasminogen activator): a protein naturally produced in the human body that helps dissolve blood clots. This substance has been created in large amounts through genetic engineering and is used to aid heart attack victims.

transgenic organism: a new organism produced by inserting genes from one species into that of another through genetic engineering

vector: the agent used to introduce foreign DNA into another cell. Common vectors are bacteria and viruses that have had foreign genes spliced into them.

xenotransplantation: the use of transgenic animals as organ donors

SOURCE NOTES

7   William J. Fulbright, *Old Myths and New Realities*, as quoted in Stephen Donadio, Joan Smith, Susan Mesres, and Rebecca La Vision, eds., *The New York Public Library Book of Twentieth Century American Quotations* (New York: Warner Books, 1992), 370.

14   Elizabeth Weise, "Life-Changing Science Began with a Humble Pea," *USA TODAY*, February 24, 2003.

15   Ibid.

20   Charles Arntzen, quoted in John Yaukey, "Public Good Is Driving Both Sides of Genetic Debate," *USA TODAY*, June 7, 2000.

20   Roger Beachy, quoted in *Of the Earth: Agriculture and the New Biology*, VHS (Washington, DC: Biotechnology Industrial Association, 1986).

22   Hope Shand, "Agricultural Biotechnology and the Public Good," speech, National Agricultural Biotechnology Council meeting, Michigan State University, East Lansing, May 23, 1994.

22   Ibid.

22   Rebecca Goldburg, Jane Rissler, Hope Shand, and Chuck Hassebrook, *Biotechnology's Bitter Harvest: Herbicide-Tolerant Crops and the Threat to Sustainable Agriculture*, Biotechnology Working Group, 1990, 10.

23   Michael N. Fox, *Superpigs and Wondercorn* (New York: Lyons & Burford, 1992), 60–61.

23–24   Ibid., 62.

24   Fred Davison, quoted in *Of the Earth*.

25   National Wildlife Federation, "A Dinner of Transgenic Foods," *Gene Exchange*, December 1, 1991, 1.

27   Jane Rissler, Union of Concerned Scientists, telephone interview with author, June 7, 1995.

28   Joseph M. Regenstein, e-mail correspondence with author, September 16, 2008.

28   Ibid.

28   Ibid.

29   Hunter Lovins, quoted in John Yaukey, "Public Good Is Driving Both Sides of Genetic Debate," *USA TODAY*, June 7, 2000.

31   Ronnie Cummins, e-mail correspondence with author, July 24, 2006.

34   Andrew Pollack, "FDA Approves Drug from Gene-Altered Goats," *New York Times*, February 6, 2009, http://www.nytimes.com/2009/02/07/business/07goatdrug.html:ref=washington (May 14, 2009).

35–36   Campaign for Responsible Transplantation, CRT, n.d., http://www.crt-online.org (May 13, 2009).

37   Vernon Jennings, "Transgenic Transgressions?" *GeneWatch*, January 1994, 5.

42   Andrew Kimbrell, *The Human Body Shop: The Engineering and Marketing of Life* (New York: HarperCollins, 1997), 183.

42   Pew Charitable Trusts, *Pew Initiative on Food and Biotechnology*, 2003, http://pewcharitabletrusts.com/pdf/biotech_poll_091303.pdf (April 23, 2009).

42   Kimbrell, 177.

44   Michael Rodemeyer, "Technology Moves Faster Than Regulators," *USA TODAY*, December 29, 2008.

44   Ibid.

47   Michael Hansen, telephone conversation with author, July 11, 2006.

48   Ibid.

48   H. Daughaday and D. M. Barbano, "Bovine Somatotropin Supplementation of Dairy Cows," *JAMA*, 1990, 1,003–1,005, as quoted in "The Pure Facts—BST and Milk," brochure, Monsanto.

54   Kathleen Fackelmann, "Mistrust of Doctors Widespread across USA; Poll Finds Many Fear Possible Experiments," *USA TODAY*, November 26, 2002.

55   Daniel Salomon, quoted in Liz Szabo, "Gene Therapy's Slow Path; What Started as a Revolution Has Run into Roadblocks," *USA TODAY*, April 5, 2005.

55   Theodore Friedmann, e-mail communication to author, July 20, 2006.

55   Ibid.

56   Ibid.

61   Council for Responsible Genetics, *Position Paper on the Human Genome Initiative* (Cambridge, MA: Council for Responsible Genetics, 1990), 2.

61   Ibid., 64.

63   American Civil Liberties Union, "Forensic DNA Databank," ACLU, March 20, 2007, http://www.aclu.org/privacy/biotech/29096res20070320.html (May 13, 2009).

63   Steve Watson, "Bush Signs Bill to Take All Newborns/ DNA," Infowars.net, May 2, 2008, http://www.infowars.net/articles/may2008/020507DNAhtm (March 24, 2009).

64   Twila Brase, "Newborn Genetic Screening: The New Eugenics?" Citizens Council on Health Care, April 29, 2009, http://www.cchconline.org/pdf/NBS_EUGENICS_REPORT_Apr2009_FINAL.pdf (May 13, 2009).

64   Bob Unruh, "National DNA Database Gets Kickstart from Feds," *World Net Daily*, May 1, 2008, http://www.wnd.com/index.php?fa=PAGE.view&pageId=63112 (March 24, 2009).

70   Ruth Hubbard and Elijah Wald, *Exploding the Gene Myth* (Boston: Beacon Press, 1993), 24–25.

70   Sarah-Kate Templeton, "Two Children Should Be Limit, Says Green Guru," *TimesOnline*, February 1, 2009, http://women.timesonline.co.uk/tol/life_ and_style/women/families/article5627634.ece (March 25, 2009).

75   Henry Desmarais, "Fears Are Overblown," *USA TODAY*, August 20, 2002.

76   Council for Responsible Genetics, "Genetic Discrimination," 2001, CRG, http://www.councilforresponsiblegenetics.org/ViewPage.aspx?pageId=85 (June 4, 2009).

76   Council for Responsible Genetics, "Genetic Testing, Discrimination and Privacy," October 12, 2007, http://www.gene-watch.org/programs/ privacy.html

77   *USA TODAY*, "More Than 1,100 Tests Look for Genetic Links to Various Diseases," Opinion Page, May 21, 2008.

80   WADA, "WADA Gene Doping Symposium Reaches Conclusions and Recommendations," The World Anti-Doping Agency, December 5, 2005, http://www.wada-ama.org/en/newsarticle.ch2?articleId=3115229 (March 21, 2009).

87   Humane Society of the United States, "Cloning of Pets: The HSUS Statement," HSUS, n.d., http://www.hsus.org/pets/issues_affecting_our _pets/hsus_statement_on_the_cloning_of_pets.html (March 23, 2009).

90–91   Alice Park, "A Talk with Dolly's Creator," *Time*, July 3, 2006, http://www .time.com/time/health/article/0,8599,1210055,00.html (March 23, 2009).

94   Pope Benedict XVI, *Dignitas Personae [Human Dignity]* (Vatican City: Congregation for the Doctrine of the Faith, December 12, 2008), http:// www.zenit.org/index.php?l=english (March 17, 2009).

95   Mimi Hall, "Ending Stem Cell Ban May Spark New Fight," *USA TODAY*, November 17, 2008.

96   Claudia Kalb, "The Whole World Is Watching," *Newsweek*, March 30, 2009, 44.

96   Stuart Newman, telephone interview with author, July 27, 2006.

96   National Institutes of Health, "Stem Cells and Diseases," NIH,May 1, 2009, http://stemcells.nih.gov/info/health.asp (May 13, 2009).

96–97   David Stout and Timothy Williams, "House Votes to Reverse Ban on Funding for Stem Cell Research," *New York Times*, May 24, 2005, http:// www.nytimes.com/2005/05/24/politics/24cnd-stem.html? _r=1&pagewanted=print (March 17, 2009).

97–98   Ken Gewertz, "Stem Cell Research Debate Continues," *Harvard News Office*, April 21, 2005, http://www.news.harvard.edu/ gazette/2005/04.21/01-stem.htm (June 4, 2009).

99   National Cable Satellite Company, *C-SPAN Congressional Chronicle*, n.d., http://www.c-spanarchives.org/congress/?q=node/77531&id=7484456 (May 13, 2009).

99   PHYSorg.com, "Obama Wants Congress to Act on Lifting Stem Cells Ban, PhsOrg.com, January 17, 2009, http://www.physorg.com/news151392818.html (January 28, 2009).

99   New York Times Company, "Obama Lifts Bush's Strict Limits on Stem Cell Research," *New York Times*, March 10, 2009, http://www.nytimes.com/2009/03/10/us/politics/10stem.html?nl=pol&emc=pola1 (June 10, 2009).

99   Ibid.

103   Stuart Newman and Nachama Wilker, "CRG Says No to Patenting Life-Forms," *GeneWatch*, July 1992, 8.

103   Ibid.

103   *Animals, People and Biotechnology* (Washington, DC: Biotechnology Industry Organization, 1992), 8.

103   Newman and Wilker.

105   Linda Nielsen and Peter Whittaker, "Ethical Aspects of Patenting Inventions Involving Human Stem Cells," The European Group on Ethics in Science and New Technologies, May 7, 2002, http://ec.europa.eu/european_group_ethics/docs/avis16_en.pdf (June 10, 2009).

110   *ETC Group Communiqué*, "Captain Hook Awards for Biopirac 2006, Issue 92, March–April 2006, http://www.etcgroup.org/documents/ETCCom.2006HOOKfinal.pdf (May 25, 2009).

110   Deb. S. Carstoiu, e-mail correspondence with author, July 21, 2006.

110   Ibid.

111   Biotechnology Industry Organization, "Why Are Patents Important to Investors?," 2008, *Science for Life*, http://bio.org/ip/primer/importance.asp (May 14, 2009).

111   *ETC Group Communiqué*.

112   Jeremy Rifkin, "Let's Stop Playing God," *USA TODAY*, May 19, 1995.

113   Warren Kaplan, "Biotech Patenting 101," *GeneWatch*, n.d., http://www.councilforresponsiblegenetics.org/ViewPage.aspx?pageId=166 (June 2, 2009).

113   James E. Rogan, "Letter to the Senate and House Apprpriations Committees," *National Right to Life*, November 20, 2003, http://www.nrlc.org/killing_embryos/Human_Patenting/patentletter112003.html (June 2, 2009).

117   Newman interview.

121   Rebecca Goldburg, Environmental Defense Fund, telephone interview with author, June 3, 1995.

122   Ibid.

123   Elizabeth Weise, "Report Urges More Regulation as Biotech Gods Hit Mainstream," *USA TODAY*, April 28, 2003.

125   Elizabeth Weise, "Label Fight Heats Up in Oregon," *USA TODAY*, October 10, 2002.

125   Daniel Bush, "ASPB Urges Opposition to Mandatory Labeling of Genetically Modified Foods in Oregon," American Society of Plant Biologists, October 2002, http://www.scienceblog.com/community/older/2001/A/f2002987.html, (April 6, 2009).

126   Jane Rissler, telephone interview with author, June 7, 1995.

126   Ibid.

126   Ibid.

126–127   PBS, "Interviews: Jane Rissler," PBS.org, October 2000, http://www.pbs.org/wgbh/harvest/interviews/rissler.html (April 7, 2009).

127   Ibid.

127   Elizabeth Milewski, telephone interview with author, June 1995.

127   Sheldon Krimsky, telephone interview with author, June 1995.

127   Ibid.

128   Ibid.

128   Ibid.

128   Michael Fernandez, telephone interview with author, July 26, 2006.

128   Ibid.

128–129   Ibid.

129   Goldburg interview.

129   GAO, "Food Labeling: The FDA Needs to Better Leverage Resources, Improve Oversight, and Effectively Use Available Data to Help Consumers Select Healthy Foods," Government Accountability Office, 2008, http://www.gao.gov/new.items/d08597.pdf (April 8, 2009).

129   Ibid.

129   Syntheticbiology.org, "Synthetic Biology Is," syntheticbiology.org, n.d., http://syntheticbiology.org (June 10, 2009).

130   ETC Group, "Global Coalition Sounds the Alarm on Synthetic Biology, Demands Oversight and Societal Debate," *ETC*, May 19, 2006, http://www.etcgroup.org/en/materials/publications.html?pub_id=8 (May 14, 2009).

130   Ibid.

130   Ibid.

131   Jack Doyle, "Corporations on Campus: Bio-Science for Sale," *Not Man Apart*, July-August 1987, 10.

131   Fred Davison, quoted in *Of the Earth*.

131   Hubbard and Wald, 160.

131   Ibid., 161.

SELECTED BIBLIOGRAPHY

Andrews, Edmund L. "Religious Leaders Prepare to Fight Patents on Genes." *New York Times*, May 13, 1995.

Angier, Natalie. "The Curse of Living within One's Genes." *New York Times*, December 18, 1994.

Ayres, B. Drummond. "Simpson Defense Seeks Role in Blood Tests." *New York Times*, July 26, 1994.

Babington, Charles. "Stem Cell Bill Gets Bush's First Veto." *Washington Post*, July 20, 2006.

Begley, Sharon, and Adam Rogers. "It's All in the Genes." *Newsweek*, September 5, 1994.

Bishop, Jerry E. "Mice Altered to Make Human Antibodies for Scientists to Use against Diseases." *Wall Street Journal*, April 28, 1994.

———. "One of First Successful Cases of Gene Put Permanently in Person Is Described." *Wall Street Journal*, April 1, 1994.

Blakeslee, Sandra. "Gene Transplant Speeds Salmon Growth Rate." *New York Times*, September 20, 1994.

Braun, David. "Scientists Successfully Clone Cat." *National Geographic News*, February 14, 2002.

Brown, Jeremy. "The Trojan Gene Hypothesis," *Fishermen's News*, March 2000.

Brownlee, Shannon. "Designer Babies." *Washington Monthly*, March 2002.

Burton, Thomas M. "Baxter Planning Research Partnership on Use of Altered Pig Organs in Humans." *Wall Street Journal*, August 30, 1994.

Carey, John, and Geoffrey Smith. "The Next Wonder Drug May Not Be a Drug." *Business Week*, May 9, 1994.

CBS News." Five Pit Bulls Cloned in South Korea." *CBS*. August 5, 2008. http://www.cbsnews.com/stories/2008/08/06/tech/main4323852. shtml (June 10, 2009).

Congressional Research Service. *CRS Report for Congress: StarLink Corn Controversy: Background*, January 10, 2001.

Cooke, Robert. "A Step Forward for Gene Therapy." *New York Newsday*, September 1, 1994.

Council for Responsible Genetics. *Genetic Engineering: Unresolved Issues*. Cambridge, MA: Council for Responsible Genetics, 1992.

———. *Genetic Testing: Preliminary Policy Guidelines*. Cambridge, MA: Council for Responsible Genetics, June 2006.

Doyle, Jack. "Biotechknowledgy Respects Nature." *Des Moines Sunday Register*, July 2, 1989.

Dudley, William, ed. *Genetic Engineering*. San Diego: Greenhaven Press, 1990.

Durfy, Sharon J., and Amy E. Grotevant. "The Human Genome Project." *Scope Note 17*. Washington, DC: National Reference Center for Bioethics Literature, Kennedy Institute of Ethics, 1991.

Of the Earth: Agriculture and the New Biology. VHS. Washington, DC: Industrial Biotechnology Association, 1986.

ETC Group Backgrounder. "Genetic Pollution in Mexico's Center of Maize Diversity" 8, no. 2, (Spring 2002).

Fox, Michael W. *The New Creation*. Washington, DC: Humane Society of the United States, 1992.

———. *Superpigs and Wondercorn*. New York: Lyons & Burford, 1992.

Frankel, Edward. *DNA: The Ladder of Life*. New York: McGraw-Hill, 1979.

Hastings Center Report. "Genetic Grammar: 'Health,' 'Illness,' and the Human Genome Project." Special supplement, July–August 1992.

Gibbs, Nancy. "Stem Cells–The Hope and the Hype." *Time*, August 7, 2006.

GlobalSecurity.org. "Artificial Spider Silk Could Improve Body Armor, Parachutes," February 28, 2008. http://www.globalsecurity.org/military/library/news/2008/02/mil-080228-afpn02.htm (June 10, 2009).

Goldburg, Rebecca, Jane Rissler, Hope Shand, and Chuck Hassebrook. *Biotechnology's Bitter Harvest: Herbicide-Tolerant Crops and the Threat to Sustainable Agriculture*. Washington, DC: Biotechnology Working Group, 1990.

Gonick, Larry, and Mark Wheelis. *The Cartoon Guide to Genetics*. New York: Barnes and Noble, 1983.

Hawkes, Nigel. *Genetic Engineering*. New York: Gloucester Press, 1991.

Hubbard, Ruth, and Elijah Wald. *Exploding the Gene Myth*. Boston: Beacon Press, 1993.

Hyde, Margaret O., and Lawrence E. Hyde. *Cloning and the New Genetics*. Hillside, NJ: Enslow Publishers, 1984.

Jaroff, Leon. "The Gene Hunt." *Time*, March 20, 1989.

Jenning, Vernon. "Transgenic Transgression?" *GeneWatch*, January 1994, 3–4.

Juma, Calestous. *The Gene Hunters: Biotechnology and the Scramble for Seeds*. Princeton, NJ: Princeton University Press, 1989.

Khor, Martin. "500,000 Indian Farmers Rally against GATT and Patenting of Seeds." *Third World Resurgence*, November 1993.

Kimbrell, Andrew. *The Human Body Shop—The Engineering and Marketing of Life*. San Francisco: HarperSanFrancisco, 1993.

Kolata, Gina. "Advisory Panel Clears Way for Trying Genetic Therapy on Cardiovascular Disease." *New York Times*, September 14, 1994.

———. *Clone: The Road to Dolly and the Path Ahead*. New York: William Morrow and Company, 1998.

———. "Genetic Approach to Preventing Regrowth of Arterial Plaque." *New York Times*, August 9, 1994.

———. "New Ability to Find Earliest Cancers: A Mixed Blessing?" *New York Times*, November 8, 1994.

———. "Strengths and Weaknesses Apparent in Two DNA Tests," *New York Times*, July 26, 1994.

Leary, Warren E. "Research Hints of Immunization via Food." *New York Times*, May 5, 1995.

Lippman, Abby. "Should We Expand Prenatal Screening?" *L'Observatoire de la Genetique*, April 2002.

Maddox, John. "Adventures in the Germ-Line." *New York Times*, December 11, 1994.

Mellon, Margaret. *Biotechnology and the Environment*. Washington, DC: National Wildlife Federation, 1988.

Micklos, David A., and Greg A. Freyer. *DNA Science*. Burlington, NC: Cold Spring Harbor Laboratory Press and Carolina Biological Supply Company, 1990.

Monsanto Company. *The New Biology: The Science and Its Applications*. Saint Louis: Monsanto Company, 1992.

Moore, Stephen D. "SmithKline Beecham Expects to See Some Gene Rights." *Wall Street Journal*, September 23, 1994.

Nature. "Fetal Gene Therapy under the Microscope." December 8, 1994.

———. "House of Lords Is Asked to Rule on Breadth of Gene Patent Coverage." December 8, 1994.

———. "More Patent Troubles about Genes." December 8, 1994.

Newman, Stuart. "My Attempt to Patent A Human-Animal Chimera." *L'Observatoire de la Genetique*, April–May 2006.

Newman, Stuart, and Nachama Wilker. "CRG Says 'No' to Patenting Life-Forms," *GeneWatch*, July 1992.

Norsigian, Judy, "Egg Donation Dangers." *GeneWatch*, September–October 2005.

Nowak, Rachel. "Forensic DNA Goes to Court with O.J." *Science*, September 1994.

Osborne, Lawrence. "Got Silk," *New York Times Magazine*, June 16, 2002.

Palca, Joe. "The Promise." *Discover*, June 1994.

Physorg.com. "Obama Wants Congress to Act on Lifting Stem Cells Ban." January 17, 2009. *PHYSorg.com*. http://www.physorg.com/news151392818.html (June 10, 2009).

Pollack, Andrew. "Patenting Life: A Special Report; 'Biological Products Raise Genetic Ownership Issues.'" *New York Times*, November 26, 1999.

Pollock, Robert. *Signs of Life—The Language and Meanings of DNA*. Boston: Houghton Mifflin Co., 1994.

Redfeather, Nancy, et al. "Protect What Is Here Now—The Fight Over Hawaii's Agricultural Heritage," *GeneWatch*, May–June 2006.

Ridgeway, James. "Robocow." *Village Voice*, March 14, 1995.

Rifkin, Jeremy. *Algeny*. With Nicanor Perlas. New York: Viking, 1983.

———. "Let's Stop Playing God." *USA TODAY*, May 19, 1995.

Rissler, Jane, and Margaret Mellon, eds. "Food Allergy Conference." *Gene Exchange*, June 1994.

———. *Perils Amidst the Promise—Ecological Risks of Transgenic Crops in a Global Market*. Cambridge, MA: Union of Concerned Scientists, 1993.

———. "Recent Workshops on Risks of Transgenic Animals," *Gene Exchange*, February 1994.

Robertson, John A. "The $1000 Genome: Ethical and Legal Issues in Whole Genome Sequencing of Individuals." *American Journal of Bioethics*, 3, no. 3 (Augst 2003): W35–W42.

Sattelle, David B. *Biotechnology in Perspective*. Washington, DC: Hobsons Publishing, 1990.

Schefter, Jim. "DNA Fingerprints on Trial." *Popular Science*, November 1994.

Seligman, Jean, and Tessa Namuth. "A Gene That Says, 'No More.'" *Newsweek*, December 12, 1994.

Shand, Hope. "Patenting the Planet." *Multinational Monitor*, June 1994.

Soble, Stacy P., ed. "Potatoes Defend Themselves against Voracious Pests." *New Bio News*, 1993.

Spaulding, Sally. "Knowing Isn't Everything." *Newsweek*, April 3, 1995.

Stammer, Larry B., and Robert Lee Hotz. "Faiths Unite to Oppose Patents on Life-Forms." *Los Angeles Times*, May 18, 1995.

Stolberg, Sheryl Gay. "The Biotech Death of Jesse Gelsinger," *New York Times Magazine*, November 28, 1999.

Suzuki, David, and Peter Knudtson. *Genethics*. Cambridge, MA: Harvard University Press, 1989.

University of Wyoming. "UW Scientist Will Examine Spider Silk Use for Sutures." News release, June 27, 2006. http://www.uwyo.edu/News/showrelease.asp?id=8959 (June 10, 2009).

U.S. Food and Drug Administration. "FDA Issues Draft Guidelines on Regulating Genetically Engineered Animals." *FDA*. September 18, 2008. http://www.fda.gov/bbs/topics/NEWS/2008/NEW01887.html (June 10, 2009).

Waldholz, Michael. "Gene-Replacement Advance May Lead to Treatment of Some Inherited Diseases." *Wall Street Journal*, April 29, 1991.

Wenner, Melinda. "Making Stem Cells from Skin." *Popular Science*. September 18, 2008. http://www.popsci.com/melinda-wenner/article/2008-09/making-stem-cells-skin?page= (June 10, 2009).

Witt, Steven C. *BriefBook: Biotechnology, Microbes and the Environment*. San Francisco: Center for Science Information, 1990.

Woodward, Kenneth L. "Thou Shalt Not Patent!" *Newsweek*, May 29, 1995.

Yousfi, Jennifer. "Monsanto Sells Off Controversial Milk-Hormone Unit to Focus on Seed Product Lines." *Money Map Press*. August 21, 2008. http://www.moneymorning.com/2008/08/21/monsanto (June 10, 2009).

RESOURCES TO CONTACT

Biotechnology Industry Organization (BIO)

1201 Maryland Avenue SW
Suite 900
Washington, DC 20024
(202) 488-9200
http://www.bio.org
BIO is the world's largest biotechnology organization. Its mission is to promote biotechnology and advocate for its member organizations—both large and small. BIO members are involved in the research and development of innovative health care, agricultural, industrial, and environmental biotechnology technologies.

The Center for Food Safety

660 Pennsylvania Avenue SE, #302
Washington, DC 20003
(202) 547-9359
http://www.centerforfoodsafety.org
This nonprofit public interest and environmental advocacy group challenges harmful methods of food production via litigation and public awareness campaigns.

Council for Responsible Genetics

5 Upland Road
Suite 3
Cambridge, MA 02140
(617) 868-0870
http://www.councilforresponsiblegenetics.org
The Council for Responsible Genetics fosters public debate about the social, ethical, and environmental implications of genetic technologies. CRG works through the media and concerned citizens to distribute accurate information and represent the public interest on emerging issues in biotechnology. CRG also publishes a bimonthly magazine, *GeneWatch*, in which more information on genetic engineering can be found.

Environmental Defense Fund (EDF)

257 Park Avenue South

New York, NY 10010

(800) 684-3322

http://www.edf.org/home.cfm

Environmental Defense Fund, or EDF (formerly known as Environmental Defense), is a U.S.-based nonprofit environmental advocacy group. The nonpartisan group is known for its work on issues including global warming, ecosystem restoration, oceans, and human health. EDF's work often advocates market-based solutions to environmental problems.

ETC Group

331 W. Main Street, Suite 307

Durham, NC 27701

(919) 688-7302

http://www.etcgroup.org

ETC Group is dedicated to the conservation and sustainable advancement of cultural and ecological diversity and human rights. To this end, ETC Group supports socially responsible developments of technologies useful to the poor and marginalized. It also addresses international governance issues and corporate power.

Food First/Institute for Food and Development Policy

398 60th Street

Oakland, CA 94618

(510) 654-4400

http://www.foodfirst.org

The purpose of the Food First/Institute for Food and Development Policy is to eliminate the injustices that cause hunger. This organization also examines the effects of genetic engineering on world hunger.

Greenpeace USA

702 H Street NW, Suite 300

Washington, DC 20001

(202) 462-1177

http://www.greenpeace.org/usa/

Greenpeace is an international nonprofit organization dedicated to protecting the environment and promoting peace through diplomacy and nonviolent conflict. Greenpeace survives on volunteerism and individual donations. By not accepting corporate or government donations, Greenpeace is able to stay more true to its mission of protecting the planet from human-inflicted degradation.

The Hastings Center

21 Malcolm Gordon Road
Garrison, NY 10524-4125
(845) 424-4040
http://www.thehastingscenter.org
The Hastings Center, founded in 1969, is an independent, nonpartisan, nonprofit bioethics research institute based in the United States. It examines essential questions in health care, biotechnology, and the environment.

The Humane Society of the United States

2100 L Street NW
Washington, DC 20037
(202) 452-1100
http://www.hsus.org
The Humane Society of the United States is the largest animal advocacy group in the nation. Mostly known for its animal adoption shelters across the country, the Humane Society also strives to prevent cruelty to animals in all aspects of U.S. society.

Human Genome Project Information

http://www.ornl.gov/sci/techresources/Human_Genome/home.shtml
This government website is dedicated to providing news and information about the Human Genome Project to the public.

Monsanto Company

800 North Lindbergh Boulevard
Saint Louis, MO 63167
(314) 694-1000
http://www.monsanto.com
The Monsanto Company is a U.S. multinational, agricultural, biotechnology corporation. Monsanto is the world's leading producer of genetically engineered seed. It is also an aggressive promoter of

genetically modified foods, herbicides, and bovine growth hormones, making it a target for environmental groups the world over.

Organic Consumers Association (OCA)

6771 South Silver Hill Drive

Finland, MN 55603

http://www.organicconsumers.org

Organic Consumers Association is an online nonprofit dedicated to the labeling of genetically modified foods. It is also an advocacy group for food safety and corporate accountability.

Union of Concerned Scientists

2 Brattle Square

Cambridge, MA 02238-9105

(617) 547-5552

http://www.ucsusa.org

Started in 1969 by students and faculty at the Massachusetts Institute of Technology, the Union of Concerned Scientists has grown into a vast network of scientists and citizens dedicated to using science-based methods to promote a healthier environment. The organization also provides in-depth articles and reports on genetic engineering.

FURTHER READING AND WEBSITES

Action Bioscience
http://www.actionbioscience.org
This site explains how genetic technologies work and then asks ethical questions about genetic engineering, cloning, and other technologies.

Bioethics Resources on the Web
http://bioethics.od.nih.gov/
This National Institutes of Health website lists many online resources to find out more about topics such as stem cell research, gene patenting, biotechnology, and more.

Cloning Fact Sheet
http://www.ornl.gov/sci/techresources/Human_Genome/elsi/cloning.shtml
The site explains the how and why of cloning.

Fridell, Ron. *Decoding Life*. Minneapolis: Twenty-First Century Books, 2005.
This book unravels the mysteries of the genome and looks at present and future applications of genetic technology.

———. *Genetic Engineering*. Minneapolis: Lerner Publications Company, 2006.
This books explains the basics of genetic engineering.

Human Genome Project Information
http://www.ornl.gov/sci/techresources/Human_Genome/home.shtml
This site is all about the HGP, with information on topics such as research and the ethical issues involved.

Image Archive on the American Eugenics Movement
http://www.eugenicsarchive.org/eugenics
Cold Spring Harbor Laboratory's website shows—in poignant pictures—the sad story of the eugenics movement in the United States, with information on topics such as sterilization laws and immigration restriction based in the flawed "science" of eugenics.

Johnson, Rebecca L. *Genetics*. Minneapolis: Twenty-First Century Books, 2006.
From selective breeding to unlocking the genetic code of DNA, this in-depth look at genetics demonstrates how scientists cracked the code of life.

Kimbrell, Andrew. *Your Right to Know: Genetic Engineering and the Secret Changes in your Food*. Berkeley, CA: Ten Speed Press, 2006.
Kimbrell discusses how more than half of the processed food in the United States contains unlabeled, genetically altered ingredients and what consumers think about this.

Maddox, Brenda. *Rosalind Franklin: The Dark Lady of DNA*. New York: Harper Perennial, 2003.
This is a biography of the woman whose research was crucial to the discovery of the structure of DNA.

Sieple, Samantha, and Todd Seiple. *Mutants, Clones, and Killer Corn*. Minneapolis: Twenty-First Century Books, 2005.
Follow the field of biotechnology from its origins in selective livestock breeding to growing human organs.

Silverstein, Alvin, Virginia Silverstein, and Laura Silverstein Nunn. *DNA*. Minneapolis: Twenty-First Century Books, 2009.
This book examines what DNA is, how heredity works, and what happens when DNA is miscopied. The book also looks at current research on DNA.

Stem Cell Information
http://stemcells.nih.gov
This National Institutes of Health (NIH) website has basic information, news, and more about stem cells.

Watson, James D. *The Double Helix: A Personal Account of the Discovery of the Structure of DNA*. New York: Touchstone, 2001.
This book was written by the codiscoverer of the structure of DNA.

Webcasts-Online Audio and Video Files about Genetics and the Human Genome Project
http://www.ornl.gov/sci/techresources/Human_Genome/education/audio.shtml
This site contains audio and video clips of shows covering topics including "Labeling Biotech Food," "Debate on Therapeutic Cloning," "Risks of Genetically Engineered Organisms," and much more.

INDEX

PHOTO ACKNOWLEDGMENTS

The images in this book are used with the permission of: Centers for Disease Control and Prevention Public Health Image Library/Hsi Liu, Ph.D., MBA, James Gathany, pp. 4–5; © Chip Somodevilla/Getty Images, p. 6; © Todd Pearson/Photographer's Choice/Getty Images, pp. 8–9; © Mary Evans Picture Library/Alamy, p. 11; © Craig Mitchelldyer/USA Today, p. 17; © Jack Gruber/USA TODAY, pp. 18–19; Front cover of leaflet published 2006 by international development charity Progressio. Photo: © Adrian Arbib/Peter Arnold, Inc, p. 23; © PHOTOTAKE Inc./Alamy, p. 26; AP Photo/ Ronen Zilberman, p. 29; © Jayne Clark/USA TODAY, p. 31; © PHILIPPE PLAILLY/ EURELIOS/Photo Researchers, Inc., p. 32; © Mark Wilson/Getty Images, p. 43; AP Photo/Simon Lin, p. 45; AP Photo/Mark Duncan, pp. 50–51; © H. Darr Beiser/USA TODAY, p. 58; © John MCCOY/AFP/Getty Images, p. 62; AP Photo/Wayne Scarberry, p. 64; © Jose Luis Pelaez Inc./Blend Images/Getty Images, pp. 68–69; © Columbia Pictures/courtesy Everett Collection, p. 71; © Saturn Stills/Photo Researchers, Inc., p. 72; © Terry Ashe/Time Life Pictures/Getty Images, p. 74; © Jake P. Bacon/USA TODAY, p. 78; © Robert Hanashiro/USA TODAY, p. 79; © Dan MacMedan/USA TODAY, pp. 82–83; AP Photo/PA/Files, p. 84; © Ted Spiegel/CORBIS, pp. 100–101; © China Photos/Getty Images, p. 108; © Geoff Tompkinson/Photo Researchers, Inc., p. 116; © Jack Hollingsworth/Photodisc/Getty Images, pp. 118–119; AP Photo/Paul Sakuma, p. 124.

Cover: © Comstock Images.

ABOUT THE AUTHOR

Linda Tagliaferro is a writer and illustrator with nearly two decades of experience. She has written non-fiction books and articles on a wide variety of topics including science and travel journalism. She has written extensively for *The New York Times* and is the award-winning author of 39 books. She speaks at schools, book stores and museums.